# HANDBOOK II

## ADVANCED
## TEACHING STRATEGIES
## FOR ADJUNCT FACULTY
*Fourth Edition*

Donald E. Greive, Ed.D.
Patricia D. Lesko, MFA

Editors

To order, contact:

The Part-Time Press
P.O. Box 130117
Ann Arbor, MI 48113-0117
(734)930-6854
orders@Part-TimePress.com
Part-TimePress.com
In Canada: ca.Part-TimePress.com

© 2016 The Part-Time Press, Inc.

ISBN 13: 978-0-940017-39-9 (paperback)
ISBN 10: 0-940017-39-3 (paperback)

Printed in the United States of America.

# Table of Contents

## Acknowledgments

While the contributions of all who provided support for *Handbook II: Advanced Teaching Strategies for Adjunct Faculty* cannot be recognized, special mention of those who contributed extensively in their time and energies is in order.

We are indebted first and foremost to the authors who have provided their expertise so that others in the profession may benefit. This book benefits immensely from the professional experience of administrators, faculty and researchers dedicated to the implementation and improvement of faculty development programs for teaching faculty.

On a personal note, we wish to thank Dr. Al Smith and Richard France for professional help and counsel along the way, Catherine Worden for the energies and efforts to "put it all together," Janet Greive and Marjorie Lesko for counsel and assistance in manuscript preparation.

Without these people and many others this publication would not have been possible.

*Don Greive & P.D. Lesko*
*Editors*

*"Now that's good coffee!"*

# TOPIC I:

## Pedagogy Versus Andragogy

### By Donald Greive

|  | **Pedagogical** | **Andragogical** |
|---|---|---|
| The Learner | • The learner is dependent upon the instructor for all learning<br>• The teacher/instructor assumes full responsibility for what is taught and how it is learned<br>• The teacher/instructor evaluates learning | • The learner is self-directed<br>• The learner is responsible for his/her own learning<br>• Self-evaluation is characteristic of this approach |
| Role of the Learner's Experience | • The learner comes to the activity with little experience that could be tapped as a resource for learning<br>• The experience of the instructor is most influential | • The learner brings a greater volume and quality of experience<br>• Adults are a rich resource for one another<br>• Different experiences assure diversity in groups of adults<br>• Experience becomes the source of self-identity |
| Readiness to Learn | • Students are told what they have to learn in order to advance to the next level of mastery | • Any change is likely to trigger a readiness to learn<br>• The need to know in order to perform more effectively in some aspect of one's life is important<br>• Ability to assess gaps between where one is now and where one wants and needs to be |
| Orientation to Learning | • Learning is a process of acquiring prescribed subject matter<br>• Content units are sequenced according to the logic of the subject matter | • Learners want to perform a task, solve a problem, live in a more satisfying way<br>• Learning must have relevance to real-life tasks<br>• Learning is organized around life/work situations rather than subject matter units |
| Motivation for Learning | • Primarily motivated by external pressures, competition for grades, and the consequences of failure | • Internal motivators; self-esteem, recognition, better quality of life, self-confidence, self-actualization |

*Source: FloridaTechNet.org*

Pedagogy is based upon the teaching of children and is synonymous with the meaning of the word "leader." Thus, traditionally, teachers have been viewed as leaders in the learning process. This role involved not only the development of learning objectives, but also the development of classroom techniques and activities which are then implemented by the class "leader." In this pedagogical model the teacher had full responsibility for making all decisions about what will be learned and how it will be learned, when it will be learned and if it has been learned (Knowles, 1990).

In 1967, 80.5 percent of entering first-year students were 18 years old, while only 13.7 percent were 19 and older. By 2006, 68.5 percent of entering students were 18, while the percentage of students 19 and older more than doubled to 29.6 percent (Pryor, Hurtado, Saenz, Santos, Korn, 2008). With the arrival of an older and more diverse student body, instructors are confronted with the task of addressing a different set of needs in the classroom. Not only do adults wish to draw upon their previous experience, but they usually come to class ready and motivated to learn. In addition, they are self-directed and may be motivated to learn for real life needs as well as self satisfaction. They are often goal-oriented and problem solvers and bring with them a need to know *why* they are learning something.

Thanks to demographic changes in the composition of the college student population the andragogical model of instruction was pioneered and adopted for use by Malcolm Knowles. Knowles based his andragogical teaching model on these newly defined characteristics of the college student which he generally calls the adult student. This andragogical model is based upon:

1. the student's need to know,
2. the learner's self concept,
3. the role of the learner's experience,
4. the readiness to learn,
5. an orientation to learning, and
6. motivation.

To accommodate the andragogical model of teaching adults, we must again examine the motivation for adult learners. Far from just earning credits to get a degree as the major motivation, 21st century students and adult learners bring with them additional needs. Often the student in today's classroom will be there to meet a social need as well as an intellectual one. Many adults will be responding to specific training or professional advancement needs and will have difficulty in adjusting to courses that do not specifically address that goal or activity (Knowles, 1990).

Accompanying this set of needs are an additional set of behaviors or conditions which may be barriers to learning. For the adult learner, these may include such things as: outside family responsibilities and activities, medical and rehabilitative problems, child care, transportation problems, and lack of confidence. These conditions make it doubly important for adjunct and part-time faculty to be aware of a learning process that accommodates rather than alienates students. An additional characteristic of the adult learner is that "they will vote with their feet" in terms of course value; that is, if their needs are not met, they will simply disappear. Thus the andragogical model of teaching positively impacts student retention.

## Pedagogy Versus Andragogy: The Debate

Andragogy has become popular both within and outside adult education circles and andragogical approaches are commonly employed in adult education, nursing, social work, business, religion, agriculture and even law. Andragogy has had its opponents as well as its proponents. Much of the controversy stems from a difference in philosophy, classification and the underlying values attached to the term adult education (Davenport & Davenport, 1985).

Some prefer to view education as a single fundamental human process and feel that even though there are differences between children and adults, the learning activities of men and women are essentially the same as those of boys and girls. Such thinkers reject andragogy as an organizing principle in adult education and perceive it as a technique. London (1973) and Elias (1979) have questioned andragogy's theoretical status, general utility, and how it is different from progressive education applied to adults. They preferred to stress the oneness or unity in education. In 1980, Knowles retreated somewhat by stating:

I am at the point now of seeing that andragogy is simply another model of assumptions about learners to be used alongside the pedagogical model of assumptions, thereby providing two alternative models for testing out the assumption as to their 'fit' with particular situations. Furthermore, the models are probably most useful when seen not as dichotomous but rather as two ends of a spectrum, with a realistic assumption in a given situation falling in between the two ends (p. 47).

He also indicated that there were occasions when andragogy might be used with children and pedagogy with adults.

McKenzie (1979) defended andragogy on philosophical grounds declaring that "the existential differences between children and adults require a strategic differentiation of education practice" (p. 257).

After a review of the experimental literature comparing andragogical and pedagogical methods, Rachal (1994) concluded: "In general, the bulk of the experimental and quasi-experimental work done to date suggests an approximate equivalence between andragogical approaches and pedagogical ones on both achievement and learner satisfaction. Ultimately, practitioners will continue to employ methods that work for them" (p. 1).

Cross (1981) described Knowles' claim that andragogy could be viewed as a unified theory of adult education as "optimistic." Hartree (1984) found that Knowles' work presented three basic difficulties for adult educators: (a) confusion between whether his theory is one of teaching or one of learning, (b) confusion over the relationship he sees between adult and child learning, and (c) ambiguity as to whether he is dealing with theory or practice. She also questioned the soundness of the basic assumptions underlying the theory or practice of andragogy.

Mohring (1989) took issue with both andragogy and pedagogy. She contended that the terms andragogy (implying the education of adults) and pedagogy (meaning the education of children) are etymologically inaccurate. Although pedagogy is derived from paid, meaning "child," from antiquity it has also stood for education in general—without reference to learners' ages. Andragogy is derived from aner, meaning adult male and not adult of either sex, therefore excluding women. In view of efforts to purge English of sexist words, she proposed the use of a new term, teliagogy. Based on the Greek teleios, meaning "adult," it would include both sexes.

## Andragogy and Student-Centered Learning

Andragogy differs from pedagogy in that it places the student at the center of the learning process and it gives emphasis to collaborative relationships among students and with the instructor. The model prescribes problem-solving activities based upon the students' need rather than the goals of the discipline or the instructor. In short, the andragogical model calls for the college teacher to become a facilitator of learning rather than a director of learning. This model is sometimes described as learner-based and learner-organized. However, one must be cautious that this does not imply that the instructor show up in class with the attitude of "what do you want to do today, gang?" In fact, the andragogical model requires more professional and quality teaching techniques and strategies than the self-directed pedagogical model.

The first step in developing andragogical teaching strategy is to create a warm and friendly classroom environment. Without open communication and a warm atmosphere, students will withdraw from the collaborative process and wait to be told what to write down so they can pass the test. Be aware that many adults are anxious about their learning experience and lack confidence, thus it is important to avoid embarrassing them or making them feel ill at ease. Activities in which the students feel confident and secure should be planned. This climate should produce a nonjudgmental atmosphere in which students share in the responsibility for their learning and are not dependent upon instructor expertise.

Important to this relationship is the first class session. The first class session will very often set the tone for the balance of the course or the program, and it should start on a healthy note. Warm and open conversation can be implemented in the first session by such activities as introductions, discussions of the goals of the course, discussions of why the students are there (with the instructor indicating why he or she is there) and the incorporation of group work or partnership. This can often be accomplished simply by eliciting a response to an ice breaker statement or a question concerning the experiences of individuals in class. It is important in the first class session that you establish yourself as a partner in learning and not the expert that has all the answers. Remember that there are many students in class who are older, less affluent, of different races or with disabilities who have not experienced support or positive classroom behavior. It is important that these individuals are connected to the rest of the students in the class and made to feel welcome. Also, it is not unusual for students to have special needs which they do not care to verbalize publicly. All students should be invited to discuss with you privately any personal needs or considerations they may have.

## Classroom Strategies

During the first class it is important to establish that although the program or course will be collaborative and cooperative, it will not be a student-run class. Make it clear, however, that classroom activities will be student-centered and not discipline-centered and that relevant participation (not irrelevant) of all students is not only welcomed but expected. Many of the techniques of andragogy are the same techniques that good instructors have been using for years. Hopefully, the day of the college instructor standing in front of a group and lecturing for an hour or more has passed.

## Conducting a Discussion

Obviously, one of the most elementary and effective methods of collaborative learning is developing a stimulating discussion. This can be implemented by asking the group refreshing questions about the assignment, listing critical points concerning the assignment or related to outside assignments, and breaking the class into small groups to reach consensus. Obviously the discussion must be facilitated in such a way that it maintains class integrity and is not general conversation.

The more students who are actively involved in their learning experience, the better the learning environment becomes. Active involvement can include: presentation by students of issues and questions of concern, panel presentations and student demonstrations of their experience or knowledge that may be related to the course being taught.

## Cooperative Learning

Cooperative learning is probably the most often used student-centered technique in the college classroom today. Sometimes called collaborative learning, it is actually one of the oldest educational techniques. Cooperative learning brings students with differing abilities together in small groups where they teach each other the concepts of the class by reinforcing the lecture and text materials. The students may either work on specific projects cooperatively or take selected quizzes and/or tests together. This process forces all students to become actively involved in all activities. For the instructor there are two significant prerequisites for good cooperative education groups—thorough planning and total commitment. As a facilitator, the instructor becomes an idea person and a resource person and may even be a mediator (Sego, 1996). For additional information on the use of cooperative learning techniques refer to Topic XI.

## Questioning

The most common activity in the traditional classroom that lends itself to the andragogical model is the formulation of good questions. Good questions can lead to active and broad student participation during the learning activity. The instructor as a facilitator reserves the right to develop such questions. A few things must be kept in mind in the development of good questions. Questions should not be posed that can be answered by simple yes or no or one-word answer, rather they are posed for the stimulation of discussion. Many times questions may require a waiting period (whether they be directed to a class or an individual) and that the allowance of a period of silence after the question is not necessarily negative. Basically there are three major types of questions:

1. **Factual Questions.** Used at appropriate times to check the background knowledge of students. These may be necessary before proceeding to the next task.

2. **Application or Interpretation Questions.** These questions should be formulated to get relationships, applications, or analysis of facts and materials.

3. **Problem Questions.** Discussion questions are used to provide students the opportunity to develop solutions to a problem or issue that may be different from that of the instructor.

A spin-off of a good questioning process will be one in which a student may ask another student or group of students for assistance in formulating an answer which could then lead to an active interaction throughout the class (McKeachie, 2010).

## Non-Participating Students

The greatest fear of instructors new to the andragogical model is that students may not respond or will remain silent. The reverse of this type of conduct is that a few students may dominate the class at the expense of others. This can often be prevented by involving the students in the activities described for the first class session. That is, reduce the students' fear of speaking to build their confidence and to make them feel that they are a contributor to the class. Sometimes it is best to have students write out their answer to a posed verbal question; thus the non-participating student can be asked simply what they have written down, or if they have developed an answer with a partner, ask one for the response and ask the other if they agree. Non-participant students can be greatly encouraged by the old technique of body language. A nod of the head, a smile or a "thanks, that's a good answer" can do wonders for a student who has never before been praised for classroom participation.

One activity, when starting the class is to have the students write a short autobiography with an option to write out a life experience they may not wish to talk about themselves but give permission to the instructor to use as a class anecdote. (Permission granted, of course).

Another technique that is effective is that of asking questions that have general answers. In this case you should feel free to call upon any student in class and accept any answer given.

Another simple but effective active technique for classroom involvement is a buzzword. In this procedure the instructor may split the class into two groups or any number of groups they wish, have them assemble and develop a hypothesis that is relevant to the course work, one application of the principle and an example of the concept.

## Conclusion

To contrast the two models discussed here Knowles describes reactive and proactive learning. In the reactive environment (pedagogy), Knowles describes the traditional course instructor as requiring the students to respect their authority, to commit to learning as a means to an end, to develop competitive relationships that require only the skills and the ability to listen uncritically, to retain information, to take notes, and to predict exam questions. Whereas the proactive (andragogical) instructional environment would include people with intellectual curiosity, the spirit of inquiry, knowledge of resources available, healthy skepticism toward authority and expertise, criteria for testing, commitment to learning which requires the ability to formulate questions answerable by data, the ability to identify data available by printed material, ability to scan quickly, ability to test data against criteria, reliability and validity and the ability to analyze data to produce answers to questions (Knowles, 1990).

**Dr. Don Greive** *is an author/editor and consultant for adjunct faculty professional development programs.*

"In Their Own Words" essays are written by administrators, tenured and non-tenured faculty members who work at a variety of two- and four-year colleges and universities. We are grateful to these educators for sharing their insights and their expertise.

## Jitters, Butterfles and Nerves

Staying up late to organize binders, notebooks, and supplies – check. Reading and re-reading my students' names to try to pronounce correctly and memorize – check. Nerves before my first lecture "in front" of the class – check. Feeling prepared to teach my first online class – ask me next week!

Having taught in the elementary and secondary classroom, I thought my days of "First Day of School Nerves" we well behind me! Nerves were only for first-year teachers and maybe a teacher who changes a grade level or school and has a new environment. How did I get here?

I landed my dream job of teaching online part-time. This is what I had worked so hard for – years in the classroom and going back to school for my Ed.D. While I was extremely excited, the nerves surprised me! I was prepared, I had the academic and professional experience, and I had experience as a student in an online classroom. So why was I so nervous?

Maybe I was nervous because I badly wanted to do a good job? I had been out of the workforce for a year on maternity leave, and I was feeling slightly "rusty." Would I be able to keep up and still be a relevant, engaging, and fun teacher?

Maybe I was nervous because I was not sure how much time was going to be required in order for me to do a good job? I had a general idea of how much time the job was going to involve, but this was one of many unknowns that I faced.

Maybe I was nervous because I was not sure how the virtual, online classroom was going to impact how I delivered instruction and related to my students? I had the training, the technology skills, and the pedagogical skills, of course, but I was unsure about the reality of really teaching and educating online.

The night of my first class, I gave myself a pep talk that was not unlike the talk I had when I was a first year teacher in the brick-and-mortar classroom! I focused on how I was prepared and to remind myself that my experience and knowledge led me to this point. I focused on how I wanted to share my experiences and knowledge with adult learners, and this helped ease my nerves.

After my first class, I was on such a natural high, I couldn't get to sleep! I was so excited! It felt so good to be "back in the classroom" with motivated, eager learners who wanted to hear what I had to say. I had so much fun! They were interested, engaged, and inviting. I could not have asked for a better experience! When I went back and listed to my lecture (a practice I recommend for all new teachers when possible), I can sense my nerves, but I don't think the students noticed it!

Well, at least they were polite enough not to say anything.

*Contributed by:* **Dr. Melissa Miller.** *She completed her Ed.D. with an emphasis in Teacher Leadership from Walden University. She holds a M.Ed. from Mary Washington University and a B.A. in Interdisciplinary Studies from Virginia Tech. Dr. Miller's professional and research interests include adult and online learning, professional development, and literacy.*

# TOPIC II:

## Teaching the Adult Student

### By Donald Greive

Much has been written in recent years concerning the continuing college student in comparison to the "traditional (adult) college student." Other than a significant age difference, however, the question may be raised, "Is there really a significant difference between 21st century students and those of former years?"

Some describe continuing students with insinuations of behavioral differences. Add to this that we can anticipate yet another generation of students, born between 1995 and 2009. Unlike X-Gens and Y-Gens, this latest cohort has yet to be labeled, but have inspired names such as "Gen Tech" and "Gen Me." Others say that such a label is no more definitive than trying to define a teenager and to stereotype teens as a single group. Those who dwell on the Generation Me concept describe the students as often bored and unmotivated, having an "attitude" toward college and resistant to disciplined study. Critics maintain that it is difficult to maintain the attention of Gen Me students thanks to their desire for immediate gratification. Critics also claim it is difficult to establish meaningful learning objectives and goals with Gen Me students.

The counter argument maintains that such students have always been present in all classrooms through all generations. Other than the age difference, other characteristics of the Generation Me student are that such students have experienced fantasy driven by YouTube, movies and television; selected without guidance their own movies, videos, and music; and have grown up surrounded by the influences of media. They have lived in the world of media entertainment and with the Internet. They have experienced a cultural environment that appears unfiltered. This environment has led to attitudes that may surface in the classroom in the form of consumer expectations and lack of respect for authority. It appears that this is a cultural behavior rather than an educational one.

In fact, on occasion these types of attitudes are expressed in confrontational rather than cooperative behavior. Although one should not err on the side of generalizing, it should be recognized that the cultural factors influencing students are unique to their cultures. As Jim Westerman writes in his essay "Toward the Best in the Academy," published by the Professional & Organizational Development Network in Higher Education: Gen Me college students "have never known a world without a television remote control, cell phones, an ATM, or the Internet. Generation Me has developed expectations for instant gratification—the Internet for information and entertainment, cell phones and instant messaging for communication.... Two-thirds of Gen Me students used computers by the age of 5, and they are exposed to an average of 8 hours of media every day (in contrast to spending 2 hours with parents and 50 minutes doing homework)."

## Classroom Implications

Realizing the challenges presented by the present student cohort, as a part-time instructor, you should be cognizant of the fact that you need to build teaching strategies and procedures that will activate the learner. Such activities include role-playing and cooperative education strategies described elsewhere in this book. It should be kept in mind that today's students will expect a certain amount of autonomy and will respond to classroom activities that they see as meaningful and in which they are involved. They will respond to topics and work assignments that may be researched and investigated on the Internet in addition to print documents and periodicals from the library. In terms of immediate gratification, they will expect answers to their questions in class and comments and notes on their tests and quizzes.

## Planning Classroom Activities

It is important that when teaching you keep in mind that these students want to *do* something rather than *know* something. Materials for class presentations should be designed to incorporate a variety of media and formats including audio, video, graphics and even Snapchat, Instagram and Twitter. In the formulation of class objectives and activities, it is not suggested that you forfeit your role; it is suggested, however, that students could be involved in describing and selecting some of the activities that they will perform in order to reach those objectives. It is important that when teaching the Me-Generation student that you remember that you are a facilitator of learning and not the final expert.

## Teaching Tips

As indicated earlier in this discussion there are significant forces at work in our environment and culture which effect the behavior of students. Although many of the traditional teaching strategies still apply, it remains that teaching is teaching and learning is learning. Jim Westerman offers the following four excellent strategies:

**Skill Variety** – Gen Me likes to multitask. They see themselves as "internal customers" and they need engagement and involvement (if not entertainment). They are active-experimentation oriented, they want to experience more than passively observe. I suggest using Socratic method and case studies when possible, building teams, holding debates, building active-engagement websites, and challenging them to use their technological skills to solve problems.

**Task Identity and Significance** – Gen Me desperately wants to feel that what they are doing is meaningful and important. Provide connections with the world that they are living in as frequently as possible to maximize the salience of your subject. Serve as a role model, and emphasize the functional benefits of learning the material every day. Explain the "why" of what you're asking them to do, and explain what's in it for them. Try to back up what you say with real-world verifiable proof. Many of them are searching for identity, and faculty could view this as an opportunity to help them to affiliate/find meaning in your classroom and subject.

**Autonomy** - Within limits, let them express individuality in their work. Be wary of one-size-fits-all teaching approaches. They often refuse to blindly conform to traditional standards and time-honored institutions. Try to provide a flexible, fun classroom and don't be too rigid. They chafe at many stepped processes and bureaucracy, and they are not so comfortable with rigid routines. Reconsider squishing them into pre-existing classroom molds, they don't want to feel like they are a cog in a boilerplate classroom. Interact with them, update your class and customize where possible. Try to enable self-expression and autonomy in the classroom.

**Feedback** - Get them involved quickly - they want to get up to speed fast and contribute. Think of the video game: expectations are clear, behavior is continually measured and feedback is consistently provided on performance, and players receive high rates of reinforcement to motivate them to keep playing. Provide frequent performance feedback (like weekly quizzes, activities and presentations in the classroom, and other high-involvement activities).

With changing attitudes and cultural influences, however, you will occasionally find yourself in a situation that is particularly challenging. Listed below are some of these situations as they relate to the Generation Y Student.

## The Aggressive Student

Aggressive students are common in the college classroom. This student will not hesitate to speak up, to question why certain things must be learned, how it's going to help and why they should do it. Many times the response that "this is a course requirement" is not sufficient. The initial response, of course, is to meet the aggressive student in an informal atmosphere during a break to try to break down barriers and direct the energies to the real purpose at hand—to assist the student in being successful in the course. If it is a particular issue in which there is sharp disagreement, you must state your position calmly and rationally and recognize that not everyone agrees with everyone else in the class, including the instructor. This can also be turned into a very positive learning experience involving the aggressive student by presenting the issues to the class by simply saying "how do the rest of you feel about this?" This can very effectively be used as an interactive tool in the classroom where small groups can meet to discuss the issues and reach a conclusion.

## The Class Expert

With the increased numbers of adults returning to higher education, many students in class may be older than the instructor and there will sometimes be situations where a class expert will surface. These students typically fall into two categories: a) the genuine expert who may in fact know more about a particular topic or issue than the instructor (this is very easy to accommodate by inviting the student to make a presentation) and b) the "know-it-all" student who feels he or she is an expert on anything at anytime. Dealing with this student sometimes leads to an argument rather than a discussion and needs to be minimized or it will distract the class. The easiest way to handle such behavior is to allow the student to express him or herself, and ask the other students for response and reaction. This will usually convey the message that his or her contribution is either of value or is wasting their time.

The final responsibility still lies with the instructor to point out the objectives of the course and to get on with the business of the class.

## The Inattentive Student

The inattentive student can take many forms. Occasionally it will be a group of two or three students who carry on their own conversation at their own pace. Occasionally it will be the student who sits with a blank facial expression as if to dare you to teach them. Many times they will respond to questions with the answer "I don't know."

To counter this behavior, several techniques are available. The first is a buzz session group where students are put together and each are asked to participate. If this does not work, the instructor may ask each student in the class to write a short paper indicating what they have observed over the last half hour of class and what they would like to see discussed. A relocation of the seating arrangement may also be effective. Finally, you must realize that a few students cannot be allowed to usurp the learning opportunities of the other students in the class. Remember the Generation Me students consider themselves consumers and customers and they expect the product to be delivered regardless of the situation.

## The Discouraged Student

Possibly the most important student for the instructor of Generation Me is the student who is challenged, insecure, and/or not confident of her/his ability to succeed even before entering the classroom. You must realize that this is not the result of your behavior, of your class preparation, or of your making. These are the students referred to in the previous discussion who may have medical or disability problems or a number of other problems to overcome. Years ago these people would not have been in college classrooms, but today they are arriving with the hope that there is some value and benefit to this experience in their lives. Anyone who has taught in the modern classroom has experienced the success stories of this type of student. Many times they are difficult to identify. The only sure method that you can incorporate to include these people is to make sure that all students are treated with the utmost respect and support and that you have an arsenal of professional techniques to address and encourage these and all students.

**Dr. Don Greive** *is an author/editor and consultant for adjunct faculty programs.*

# TOPIC III:

## 101 Strategies You Can Use During the First Weeks of Class

Beginnings are important. Whether it is a large introductory class for freshmen or an advanced course in a major field, it makes good sense to start the semester off well. Students will decide very early – some say the first day of class – whether they will like the course, its contents, the teacher, and their fellow students.

The following list of "101 Strategies You Can Use..." is offered in the spirit of starting off right. It is a catalog of suggestions for college teachers who are looking for fresh ways of creating the best possible environment for learning. Not just the first day, but the first three weeks of a course are especially important, studies say, in retaining capable students. Even if a syllabus is printed and lecture notes are ready to go the week before class, most college teachers can usually make adjustments in teaching methods as the course unfolds and the characteristics of their students become known.

These suggestions have been gathered from college and university faculty at several institutions. For many faculty, much of this is "old hat." But even for long-time teachers, there may be that one jewel of a suggestion that may help get you off on the right foot. The rationale for these methods is based on the following needs:

- **To help students make the transition** from high school and, in August, summer activities to learning in college;

- **To direct students' attention** to the immediate situation for learning – the hour in the classroom;

- **To spark intellectual curiosity** – to challenge students;

- **To support beginners** and neophytes in the process of learning in the discipline;

- **To encourage the students' active involvement** in learning; and

  ❧ **To build a sense of community** in the classroom.

Here, then, are some ideas for college teachers to use in their courses at the beginning of the term.

## Helping Students Make Transitions

1.  **Hit the ground running** on the first day of class with substantial content.

2.  **Take attendance**: roll call, clipboard, sign in, seating chart.

3.  **Introduce yourself** by short presentation, or self-introduction.

4.  **Provide** an informative, interactive, and user-friendly **syllabus**. Post all materials online.

5.  **Give an assignment** on the first day to be collected at the next meeting.

6.  **Start laboratory experiments** and other exercises the first time lab meets.

7.  **Call attention (written and oral) to what makes good lab practice**: completing work to be done, procedures, equipment, clean up, maintenance, safety, conservation of supplies, full use of lab time.

8.  **Give a learning style inventory** to help students find out about themselves.

9.  If your campus has one, **direct students to the Academic Success Center** for help on basic skills.

10. **Tell students how much time they will need to study** for this course.

11. **Hand out supplemental study aids**: library hours, study best practices, supplemental readings and exercises.

12. **Explain how to study** for the kind of tests you give.

13. **Put in writing a limited number of ground rules** regarding absence, late work, testing procedures, grading, and general decorum, and maintain these.

14. **Announce office hours** frequently and hold them without fail.

15. **Show students how to handle learning in large classes** and impersonal situations.

16. **Give sample test questions.**

17. **Give sample test answers.**

18. **Explain the difference between legitimate collaboration and academic dishonesty;** be clear when collaboration is wanted and when it is forbidden.

19. **Seek out a different student each day** and get to know something about him or her.

20. **Ask students to write about what important things** are currently going on in their lives.

21. **Find out about students' jobs:** if they are working, how many hours a week and what kind of jobs they hold.

## Directing Students' Attention

22. **Greet students at the door** when they enter the classroom.

23. **Start class on time.**

24. **Make a grand stage entrance** to hush a large class and gain attention.

25. **Give a pre-test** on the day's topic.

26. **Start the lecture with a Tweet, audio/video clip, puzzle, question, paradox, picture or cartoon** to focus the day's topic.

27. **Elicit student questions and concerns** at the beginning of the class and list these on the chalkboard to be answered during the hour.

28. **Have students write down what they think the important issues** or key points on the day's lecture will be.

29. **Ask a person who is reading the student newspaper what is in the news today.**

## Challenging Students

30. **Have students write out their expectations** for the course and their goals for learning.

31. **Use variety in methods of presentation** every class meeting.

32. **Stage a figurative "coffee break"** about 20 minutes into the hour: tell an anecdote, invite students to put down their pens and pencils, refer to a current event, shift media.

33. **Incorporate community resources**: plays, parks, concerts, the County Fair, government agencies, businesses, the outdoors.

34. **Show a film in a novel way**: stop it for discussion, show a few frames only, anticipate the ending, hand out a viewing or critique sheet, play and replay parts.

35. **Share your philosophy of teaching** with your students.

36. **Form a student panel** to present alternative views of the same concept.

37. **Stage a "change-your-mind" debate**, with students moving to different parts of the classroom to signal change in opinion during the discussion.

38. **Conduct a "living" demographic survey** by having the students move to different parts of the classroom: size of high schools, rural vs. urban, consumer preferences.

39. **Tell about your current research interests** and how you got there from your own beginnings in the discipline.

40. **Conduct a role-play** to make a point or lay out issues.

41. **Let your students assume the role of a professional** in the discipline: philosopher, literary critic, biologist, agronomist, political scientist, engineer.

42. **Conduct idea-generating and brainstorming sessions** to expand horizons.

43. **Give students two passages of material containing alternative views** to compare and contrast.

44. **Distribute a list of the unsolved problems,** dilemmas, or great questions in your discipline and invite students to claim one as their own to investigate.

45. **Ask students what books they read** over the summer.

46. **Ask students what is going on in the state legislature** on a subject which may affect their future.

47. **Let your students see the enthusiasm** you have for your subject and your love of learning.

48. **Take students with you** to hear guest speakers or special programs on campus.

49. **Plan a "teaching professional" lesson** or unit which shows students the excitement of discovery in your discipline.

## Providing Support

50. **Collect students' current cell phone numbers and email addresses** and let them know that you may need to reach them.

51. **Check out absentees.** Email or text.

52. **Diagnose the students' prerequisite learning** by a questionnaire or pre-test and give them feedback as soon as possible.

53. **Hand out study questions** and study guides.

54. **Be redundant.** Students should hear, read and see key materials at least three times.

55. **Allow students to demonstrate progress in learning**: summary quiz over the day's work, a written reaction to the day's material.

56. **Use non-graded feedback** to let students know how they are doing: post answers to ungraded quizzes and problem sets, exercises in class, verbal feedback.

57. **Reward behavior you want**: praise, stars, personal note.

58. **Use a light touch**: smile, tell a good joke, break test anxiety with a sympathetic comment.

59. **Organize**. Give visible structure by posting the day's "menu" on the chalkboard or overhead.

60. **Use multi-media**: text, audio, video, animation, graphics.

61. **Use multiple examples, in multi-media**, to illustrate key points and important concepts.

62. **Make appointments** with all students (individually or in small groups).

63. **Hand out wallet-sized telephone cards** with all important telephone numbers listed: office, department, resource centers, teaching assistant, lab.

64. **Print all important course dates** on a card that can be handed out and taped to a mirror.

65. **Eavesdrop on students before and after class** and join their conversations about course topics.

66. **Maintain an open lab grade book,** with grades kept current, during lab time so that students can check their progress.

67. **Check to see if any students are having problems** with any academic or campus matters and direct those who are to appropriate offices or resources.

68. **Tell students what they need to do to receive an "A"** in your course.

69. **Stop the world to find out** what your students are thinking, feeling and doing in their everyday lives.

## Encouraging Active Learning

70. **Have students write something**.

71. **Have students keep a three-week three-times-a-week journal** in which they comment, ask questions and answer questions about course topics.

72. **Invite students to critique each other's essays or short answer questions** on tests for readability or content.

73. **Invite students to ask questions** and wait for the response.

74. **Probe student responses** and question their comments.

75. **Put students into pairs or "learning cells"** to quiz each other over material for the day.

76. **Give students an opportunity** to voice opinions about the subject matter.

77. **Have students apply subject matter** to solve real problems.

78. **Give students red, yellow, and green cards** (made of posterboard) and periodically call for a vote on an issue by asking for a simultaneous show of cards.

79. **Roam the aisles of a large classroom** and carry on running conversations with students as they work on course problems (a portable microphone helps.)

80. **Ask a question directed to one student** and wait for an answer.

81. **Place a suggestion box** in the rear of the room and encourage students to make written comments every time the class meets.

82. **Do oral "show-of-hands" multiple-choice tests** for summary, review and instant feedback.

83. **Use task groups** to accomplish specific objectives.

84. **Grade quizzes and exercises in class** as a learning tool.

85. **Give students opportunity for practice** before tests.

86. **Give a test early in the semester** and return it graded in the next class meeting.

87. **Have students write questions** on index cards to be collected and answered the next class period.

88. **Make collaborative assignments** for several students to work together on.

89. **Assign written paraphrases and summaries** of difficult reading.

90. **Give students a take-home problem** relating to the day's lecture.

91. **Encourage students to bring current news items** to class which relate to the subject matter and post these on a bulletin board nearby.

## Building Community

92. **Learn names.** Make an effort to learn names.

93. **Set up a buddy system** so students can contact each other about assignments and coursework.

94. **Find out about your students** via questions on an index card.

95. **Solicit student photos related to course work** and post in classroom, office or lab.

96. **Arrange helping trios of students** to assist each other in learning.

97. **Form small groups for getting acquainted**; mix and form new groups several times.

98. **Assign a team project early in the semester** and provide time to assemble the team.

99. **Help students form study groups** to operate outside the classroom.

100. **Solicit suggestions from students** for outside resources and guest speakers on course topics.

## Feedback on Teaching

101. **Gather student feedback** in the first three weeks of the semester to improve teaching and learning.

*Used with permission, Teaching and Learning Center, University of Nebraska, Lincoln, NE.*

"In Their Own Words" essays are written by administrators, tenured and non-tenured faculty members who work at a variety of two- and four-year colleges and universities. We are grateful to these educators for sharing their insights and their expertise.

## Want to Be an Inspiring Teacher? Answer This Question: "Why Do You Teach?"

Your work as an adjunct instructor – do you remember how it all began? What initially inspired you to teach? Do you still feel the same today? If you have been teaching for any length of time you probably have a familiar routine established. You understand what's expected for your instructional duties and the importance of developing an effective time management plan. You also realize that there is a significant commitment of time required to be actively engaged in the class and create a meaningful learning experience for your students. But if you find that your work has become too routine feeling, perhaps this is a good time to review the source of your inspiration and how it can have a direct impact on your performance.

Many adjuncts describe teaching as something they are passionate about and it results from a desire to share their knowledge and experience with students. It is also an opportunity to help students develop academic skills, self-motivation, self-confidence, and an overall sense of self-empowerment. Another reason why adjuncts pursue teaching opportunities is that they love to learn. Schools encourage continued learning because they expect instructors to remain current in their field and participate in professional development to expand their knowledge and enhance their facilitation skills.

Students can pick up on how you feel about teaching or your general attitude – whether you teach in a classroom or online. It is evident in the tone of your communication and responsiveness to them. If you can remember why you chose this work, despite deadlines, expectations, frustrations, and a busy (often stressful) work schedule (that may seem unrealistic to you at times), you can stay focused on what is most important to you and your students.

## Share Your Knowledge

A source of inspiration may be a desire to share knowledge and experience with students. Most adjuncts are working in a career that is related to the subject matter taught, along with advanced education. This adds depth to the class discussions because you understand the course concepts and can translate theory in a way that allows your students to view it in the context of the real world. In other words, you bring the course materials to life.

The knowledge you possess also strengthens the class assignments because you know if students are on the right track with their analyses, research and projects. For example, undergraduate students often submit written assignments that address real world issues from a "should" or "needs to" perspective, without considering the potential implications or reality of their proposed solutions. Through the use of Socratic questioning and feedback, which challenges the premise of their statements, you are able to guide students and encourage them to explore alternative perspectives, ideas, and solutions.

## Teach Skillset Development

Another source of inspiration may be the result of wanting to help students acquire more than content-specific knowledge. Adjuncts often see their students as individuals and take an interest in learning about their needs. As you know, there isn't one set of characteristics or qualities that can be applied to all students because each possess an individualized approach to learning and have varying skills and abilities. The process of teaching involves being able to quickly assess and interpret where each student stands, from an academic skill set perspective, and knowing how to assist them.

Working with students requires patience, emotional intelligence and strong communication skills – if you are going to connect with them and develop productive working relationships. Addressing skillset developmental needs such as writing and critical thinking can be very rewarding because you watch a shift in their perspectives and approaches to interacting with their environment. This is the essence of self-empowerment – when students understand that their work and effort produce a positive result, including the accomplishment of their goals.

## Encourage Lifelong Learning

Do you have a love of learning? Another reason why adjuncts choose to teach is that they are passionate about their career and enjoy reading about research, topics and trends within that field. As an educator it is absolutely essential to stay up-to-date so your instructional approach is relevant to current issues and topics. Your passion for learning will also teach your students to become lifelong learners. Encourage them to do more with their discussion responses and written assignments than offer opinions – ask them to find scholarly sources and credible information. This will also promote the development of critical thinking and analysis skills.

As you reflect upon the reasons why you are inspired to teach you are likely to remember the sense of personal and professional fulfillment that results from helping students reach their academic goals. While the work of an adjunct often requires a substantial investment of time, it is a necessary part of the process of teaching that you accept and gladly perform for the benefit of your students. The opportunity to share knowledge and experience, while teaching self-developmental skills, can be transformative for you and your students.

*Contributed by* **Dr. Bruce Johnson.** *Dr. J has a master's in Business Administration and a Ph.D. in the field of adult education. Dr. J works as an online adjunct instructor, faculty developmental workshop facilitator, and faculty mentor.*

# TOPIC IV:

## Developing the Environment for Learning

### By Helen Burnstad

Change is rapidly altering the face of post-secondary education. Technology, increased competition, more student demands, account-ability efforts, and consumerism have generated a reconsideration of the teaching/learning enterprise. Within the past five years, the Learning College movement has advocated a change of focus in the classroom—from the focus on the teacher delivering content to the student learning it. This change of focus has caused many faculty members, administrators and staff developers to consider what elements create a classroom climate that encourages more student responsibility for learning. Student needs and interests are considered as mindfully as teacher attitudes. In order to create a learning environment four areas should be examined:

1. teachers' expectations,
2. teacher and teaching behaviors,
3. physical classroom space, and
4. strategies used to create the environment for learning.

### Teacher Expectations

Each teacher should have a clear picture of his or her own style and expectations. A variety of recommendations can be found in the literature. On the one hand, writers recommend that you know your own learning style, using whichever learning style instrument you select—the 4-Mat system, Kolb, Dunn or others—since your learning style most likely contributes to choices you make about how to teach. Others suggest you know your work behavioral style, determined by using a learning tool such as the Personal Profile System from Carlson Learning Company, or your personality type using the Myers-Briggs Type Indicator. These many tools will help you be clearer about your teaching style. Student feedback may also be a way of gaining insight into your style.

Recent attention has been given to teaching as a "calling" or "art" rather than a science. Parker Palmer in his book, *The Courage to Teach*,

> takes teachers on an inner journey toward reconnecting with their vocation and their students—and recovering their passion for one of the most difficult and important of human endeavors. "This book builds on a simple premise: good teaching cannot be reduced to technique, good teaching comes from the identity and integrity of the teacher" (cover flap, 2007).

Teachers need to know themselves and their style.

A second area to consider is the teacher's teaching goals. Using the "Teaching Goals Inventory and Self-Scorable Worksheet" (http://www.Part-TimePress.com/Teaching_Goals_Inventory.pdf), a faculty member can reflect on his or her purposes for the course. This information helps to frame your philosophy and intent regarding the content of the course.

Once a faculty member has given consideration to the dimensions of both art and goals, the challenge is to present your expectations to your students. Students want and need to know their teacher and their teacher's passion for the subject area. As a faculty member, share that information with your students!

## Teacher Behavior

Classroom climate includes your presence in the classroom. Students want to know if you love your subject area — why? how?—as well as know that you like them. A pleasant persona is helpful. Enthusiasm demonstrated through energetic and engaging activities are desirable as well.

It goes without saying that preparation is paramount in communicating expectations to students. Be clear about your belief in them and their capability of learning the information in your class. You are a "significant other" for your students. If you communicate an expectation that the class will be wonderful, the learning will be engaging, and you'll all work hard together, you have established an expectation that your students will strive to meet. On the other hand, if you present them with an expectation of difficulty and predict that one half of them will fail the course, you've set their expectations as well. Being positive serves as a motivator for students.

Your expectations should also extend to how you wish your students to interact with one another. If you intend to use cooperative learning structures or team work, being clear about your expectations of the students is also important.

You may extend your expectations by explaining your teaching philosophy. What do you want your students to learn? How will you help them be successful? How does your classroom look "different" from other classrooms?

## Classroom Arrangement

The classroom you have been assigned may dictate how flexible you can be with the seating, the focus of attention, or the use of technology. If you are in a fixed-seat room, you will have to work within some confines but even that should not deter you from using variety in your classroom. Application of an understanding of learning principles such as attention span, need for change of focus, reinforcement, time on task, and processing strategies should encourage you to ask students to move, interact, ask questions, respond to one another, work quietly on tasks, listen respectfully to each other and challenge assumptions.

## Classroom Strategies for Creating a Positive Climate

- **Arrange the classroom to establish eye contact** between and among students and you. A circle or horseshoe will work nicely.

- **Introduce yourself to your students.** Be sure they know who you are, what the class is, why you are teaching the course, what background you bring to the classroom, how excited you are to share the semester with them. Make them feel comfortable and welcome.

- Be prepared for the possibility of **having students of very diverse backgrounds**. Capitalize on age differences. Mix groups so older students are with younger ones; non-native speakers of English are with native speakers, races are mixed or ability levels are combined.

- **The more actively involved students are** from the very first meeting, the better the chance of having students become comfortable in your classroom and expect to continue to be active.

- **Use a strategy for getting to know your students**. A 5" x 8" note card works very well to have students tell you about themselves. Questions might include what their major is, why they are taking the class, what their goals are for the class, what grade they intend to earn. You might also use this strategy to uncover any concerns they may have about the class, their history or past experience with the subject area, or if they are in need of any type of accommodation.

- **Learn each student's name**. Ask students what they would like to be called in class. The name on the roster may not be the name they go by. Be open to that information. Learn to pronounce the names of students correctly. Foreign names may be a challenge, but do all you can to learn each name.

- **Provide ways for students to get to know one another**. Use name tags, name plates, a roster, a "get acquainted" activity or two or dyadic interviews and introductions.

- **Prepare a complete and lively syllabus**. Include in your syllabus a statement of your teaching philosophy, or your expectations of them, or a statement of civility and behavior, or a statement of respect, or all of the above!

- **Share with students how you visualize their role in the class**. Perhaps have students establish the ground rules for the class. They will include in the ground rules the same things you would say, i.e. come prepared, come on time, be open to sharing with others, be respectful, listen carefully and other expectations for a good learning environment.

- **Have your students from a previous class "Leave a Legacy."** Ask students to write a letter or set of recommendations to your students for the next semester. The students will tell the new class everything they have learned about being successful in your class. Their voice will convey the need to be prepared, keep up with the assignments, follow directions, read, and interact. These Legacies serve to remove the "heavy-handed" sound of some requirements from your mouth. You will be encouraged by what students say!

- **Use Classroom Assessment Techniques (CATs)** to continually get feedback from your students. "The One Minute Paper" or "Muddiest Point" strategies will keep the communication flowing between you and your students.

- **If you ask for feedback, feed the information back to them.** If they ask questions, respond to them. A "no" is better than no response.

- **Invite students to confer with you early and often.** Set up a system of email contact. Be sure they know your office hours. You may even design a strategy where they must come to see you in your office.

- **Maintain an open grade book policy.** Student should know how they are doing in your class throughout the semester.

- **Give students opportunities for input into the course.** How can they share readings, videos, Internet sites, or other resources that could contribute to the content of the course? Encourage them to learn your subject matter outside of class. And apply it!

- **Be alert to how students are responding.** Read nonverbal feedback as much as possible. If you are engaged and sensitive, students will mirror that behavior as well.

- **Be confident in your role.** You are the content expert, that is why you were hired to teach this class.

### ✍ Have fun!

What you want to do to develop the environment for learning is create the classroom climate which motivates students to learn your content. These recommendations will help you do that. Consider your expectations, your philosophy, your physical setting, and the strategies you wish to use to ensure your students' success. Your students will live up—or down—to your expectations.

**Dr. Helen Burnstad** *is the Director Emeritus of Staff Development, Johnson County Community College, Overland Park, KS.*

"In Their Own Words" essays are written by administrators, tenured and non-tenured faculty members who work at a variety of two- and four-year colleges and universities. We are grateful to these educators for sharing their insights and their expertise.

## The First Class: What to do After the Introductions

After all the preparation and trepidation, the "big moment" arrives—the first class. Beyond knowledge of the content and of teaching strategies, here are some general recommendations to apply to that first class. Most of the recommendations focus upon classroom management strategies that can apply to any level of instruction.

To be successful on the first day, **BE ORGANIZED.**

1. **Organize your presentation.** Prepare a step-by-step outline to prompt you. Use media support, such as a PowerPoint presentation, to keep yourself on track.

2. **Organize your materials.** Prepare your handout materials, such as your syllabus, prior to the first class. Ensure that they are copied in time and ready to distribute during the first class. Distribute the materials in a planned and deliberate fashion, not as an afterthought.

3. **Organize your environment.** If you require audio-visual/multimedia equipment, make certain that it is scheduled and available. If you want to rearrange the classroom, do so prior to the class (if the room is not in use) or at the beginning of the class as students arrive.

4. **Organize your "Class Procedures."** If assigned seating is important to you, start the procedure during the first class. If homework assignments should be submitted at the beginning (or end) of the class into a "Homework Folder," inform the students.

And don't forget to **BE OPTIMISTIC**.

1. **Maintain optimism and a good attitude** toward your teaching and your students.

2. **Learn something about the students.** Have the students complete a form, sharing information (such as their major, favorite book, goals for enrolling in the class.) The activity can lessen their apprehension, as well as assist you in learning their names. It may also aid you in identifying student goals or needs.

You must have everything ready to go when class begins. Your success during the school year will be determined by what you do during the first class after the introductions.

*Contributed by:* **Swen H. DiGranes,** *Professor of Education at Northeastern State University, Tahlequah, OK and* **Jo Lynn Autry-DiGranes** *of Connors State College, Warner and Muskogee, OK.*

# TOPIC V:

## Connecting with the Adult Learner

By Anita C. R. Gorham and Joseph C. Gorham

Why am I here ... at this place ... at this time? Many of us have asked this question at some point in our lives. The adult learner is no exception. While most times the question is more global, many adult learners are focusing on "why am I in college at this time in my life?" While the reasons may be as varied as the cultural backgrounds and experiences of the adult learner, the answers for all will fall into one or two categories: career advancement/maintenance or self fulfillment.

As educators of adult learners, it is a part of our responsibility as facilitator to understand the backgrounds of our students. Unlike the traditional student, they have made many life choices which have broadened their experiential base, resulting in their current educational pursuit. In many cases, their need may overshadow their values. Their values may dictate that family is first, my children should be the priority; however, because of my responsibilities, I must work and my employer is mandating that I get a degree. Many are in a constant state of juggling responsibilities and attempting to be all things to many people and entities. Their priority may very well NOT be school, but again their need has become the priority: the need to stay in the race, the need to maintain their position of provider, the need to be a role model and encourage their children.

You're no doubt saying to yourself, "this all sounds very familiar, but what does it have to do with me? How does knowing this assist me in connecting effectively with the adult learner?" While it is true the adult learner may not know all the theory behind their experiences, it in no way diminishes the fact that they have had these experiences. It is our responsibility as facilitators to develop a style of integrating practicality with the theoretical aspects of learning.

Adults are motivated to invest in higher education for a myriad of reasons. Whatever the individual reasons, importance is placed on the application of the concept and not the concept itself. Because their value system is already established, the information must be presented in a manner that allows them room to integrate it into their conceptual truth.

What you see is not necessarily what you get. Because of their many experiences, responsibilities and perceptions, adult learners may be reluctant to take unnecessary risk. In most cases, their egos are well entrenched as well as their need to be in control. They have "tried and true" behavior that has helped them assimilate and thus be accepted. We, as facilitators, must create a "safe environment" that will encourage a respectful participatory exchange. We must balance respect of the student's experiences while maintaining control over the process. This necessitates that our egos are secure! We must be willing to take the risk of being challenged, thus relinquishing some control to gain more control. We must understand that they, like us, are a composite of their culture, gender and experience.

Many minority adult learners enter the educational arena from an experiential base that has been tried and tested by racism. Hence, it is important for the facilitator to be cognizant and sensitive to this reality. Viewed from this perspective, it can be said that many minority adult learners enter the classroom "sensitive" to and "expecting" to encounter some form of "institutionally structured racism." How the minority student copes with his or her place in an educational arena that is "perceived" as being racist or potentially racist or supporting racism, is to a degree contingent upon how aware and sensitive the facilitator is to the issue. In general, sensitivity is the ability to perceive with some accuracy what others think and feel.

In an effort to be sensitive to and empathetic toward the minority adult learner on the issues of race, it is essential that the faculty member **not** approach the issue by suggesting mundane and inappropriate solutions such as these:

- Minorities deserve more gains than they have attained, but because gains come at the cost of others, it is unlikely that more will be forthcoming.

- ❧ Being aware of how changing standards for the sake of educating minorities is detrimental to non-minorities.

- ❧ Although inequities exist, minorities must move to clean their own slate rather than wait for institutions to provide for them; i.e. the "boot strap approach."

- ❧ Suggesting that race issues are a result of difficulties and misunderstandings stemming from diminished and poor communication, as opposed to focusing on the possibility of racism being part of the value system that serves the purpose of the individual purporting some aspect of racism.

It is imperative that facilitators realize that a certain number of minority students will enter the classroom with a perspective that has been structured by past and current experiences of racism (or what appears to them to be racism). It is necessary for the facilitator to have the ability to sense what a student might feel, verbalize, and ultimately act upon.

The following represent some aspects of sensitivity that facilitators might want to be aware of:

- ❧ How and in what manner a facilitator makes favorable or unfavorable ratings of others.

- ❧ One's ability to suspend judgment, not jump to conclusions and demonstrate the ability to be objective from one situation to another.

- ❧ The ability to feel and communicate empathy and at the same time, keep the facilitator/student relationship clear.

- ❧ Possessing a clear understanding of personality traits.

- ❧ Through accurate observation, stereotyping is avoided.

How can we as facilitators make the connection? While there are many roads to the same destination, the following represent some highlights of our collective 20 years of experience teaching the adult learner:

- ❧ **Teach where your students are.** Because of their accumulated experience, adults are generally sensitive, goal oriented, highly motivated and self directed. Be aware of the psychological, emotional, cultural and career locale of the student.

- **What's in it for me?** Material and delivery style must be viewed by the adult learner as relevant and have immediate utilitarian value.

- **Is it safe?** The facilitator must structure an environment that is adult learner friendly in all aspects of the process.

- **Teach others as you would want to be taught.** The adult learner wants to be respected, validated and would like to view the facilitator as being objective.

- **Learning, like life, is what you make of it.** The facilitator must motivate the adult learner to be an active, responsible participant in their learning process.

**Anita C. R. Gorham** *is the Associate Director for Executive and Professional Development, Part-time Faculty and Faculty mentor, Central Michigan University, Troy, MI.*

**Joseph C. Gorham** *is a part-time faculty member at Central Michigan University, guest lecturer at several universities in the Metropolitan Detroit area, and Director of Clinical Social Work at a major Employee Assistant Program (EAP) Corporation.*

"In Their Own Words" essays are written by administrators, tenured and non-tenured faculty members who work at a variety of two- and four-year colleges and universities. We are grateful to these educators for sharing their insights and their expertise.

## Named After a Saint:

## Free Writing in the College Classroom

It took me a long time to ask my father one simple question: Would he be hurt if I legally changed my middle name when I turned eighteen? He was quiet for several minutes, time I spent worrying, Did I totally offend him? Then finally, he asked, "Exactly what is your middle name?"

My sister and I have told this story many times since then, but every time I tell it I am reminded of how important our names are. As an adjunct professor at five colleges in the Seacoast region of New Hampshire and southern Maine, I taught approximately two classes every eight weeks. Most classes were about 20 students, and it was next to impossible for me to remember students' names, especially unusual names or names I found hard to pronounce. Because I tried to learn names by week two, I had to employ a variety of techniques to be successful.

My most successful name activity came from my colleague Jennifer Miller who, near the start of each semester, asks students to free write about their names: what it means, how they feel about it, and how they got it. After the free writing time is up, Jennifer asks her students to read their free writing out loud.

When this fairly painless activity was over, I'd accomplished several things. First of all, most students will read this free write out loud; it's a safe topic about which they are an expert. So, right from the first week of classes, they participated. And what's more—this activity can be easily reworked, depending on the class. In my business communications classes, instead of a free writing activity, I asked students to write me a properly formatted memo about their names. In my composition classes, stories from this activity often turn into personal narratives.

This activity also gave me an opportunity to connect with students over a non-graded piece of writing. At the end of the class, I collected these free writes, and wrote lots of encouraging comments on them. (Since they were free writes, I didn't check for spelling, grammar, structure—all that stuff). My goal was to set a tone for the semester, especially in my larger classes where I may not have gotten to talk one-on-one with my students frequently.

And the bottom line is that I learned something about my students, something I used to remember names. One student wrote, "It's fair to say I don't just dislike my full given name, I cringe at it." Another hated her name because when it's said fast with a New England accent it sounds like "calamari." Another student was supposed to be a boy—disappointed she wasn't, her parents simply added an "a" to the first and middle names they had picked for their "son." Yet another student, last in a long line of kids, was named after a character in a movie. "There are seven children, so I would assume it was tougher after the first few," my student wrote, "my middle name, Joseph, was given for religious reasons. Each of my siblings also have (sic) middle names that are names of saints in the Catholic church."

Catholic saint-inspired or not, my students' names stuck with me as the short semester swirled by, thanks to their free writes. Indeed, maybe I should've suggested this activity to my father ... but then again, I think I tortured him enough.

*Contributed by:* **Darcy Wakefield.** *She earned her MA from SUNY/ Buffalo in 1996, and her MFA from Emerson in 2003. From August 1999 until January 2004, she taught English at Southern Maine Community College, Portland, ME.*

# TOPIC VI:

## Student Engagement: Why It Matters

By Dr. Bruce Johnson, MBA, Ph.D.

## Student Retention—Why It Matters

When you hear the phrase "student retention," what comes to mind? A set of numbers beyond your control? It is easy to view student retention, student satisfaction, and student persistence as a responsibility of college or university administrators. The truth of the matter is that student retention is one of the most widely studied areas in higher education. In the 1970s, student retention was seen as a reflection on the individual student, her/his skills, and work ethic. College drop-outs were thought to be less able and less motivated. Students failed, not institutions.

Over the course of the past decades, that perception has changed dramatically. For example, our understanding of the experience of students of different educational, social and economic backgrounds has grown. Throughout these changes, one fact has remained clear: involvement, or what is commonly referred to as engagement, matters and it matters most during the critical first year of college. Part-time faculty are more likely to be employed to teach first year students, and so become important players in any institution's student engagement and retention efforts.

These classrooms, staffed part-time instructors who are (ideally) well-supported by the school, are where students are first engaged in the college learning experience. It is now a widely accepted fact that classroom faculty are key to institutional efforts to increase student retention. We are often reminded that student retention is everyone's business. However, research has made it clear that student retention is the business of the faculty in particular.

## Students Make the First Choice

When a student decides to attend a particular school, it is often because of an interest in a specific degree program. As a means of attracting new students, schools promote programs, resources, services, features and other opportunities. Students often make an initial decision based upon their expectations of what they hope to accomplish and learn by earning their degrees. The reality of these expectations comes to light when students step into their classrooms and meet their instructors—meet you.

## Instructors Reaffirm or Negate that Choice

The classroom environment an instructor creates helps students confirm, discard or adapt their expectations about the process of learning. When an instructor is responsive, students are likely to believe their developmental needs can be met. Instructors who create meaningful learning environments encourage student retention. However, the goal is not simply to keep students enrolled in their degree programs, but rather to focus on educational outcomes— where students create knowledge and develop skill sets through active participation in the process of learning. Student retention is sometimes an issue of persistence, because students may face significant challenges—such as academic preparedness, time management and self-motivation.

## Retention is More than Numbers

From a developmental perspective one of the most important issues with respect to student retention is sustained growth—the student's ability to develop skill sets and acquire knowledge. From the student's perspective, there is an expected return on investment of time, effort and, of course, money. Student retention involves positive learning experiences and interactions with instructors. Recent research indicates that part-time faculty at community colleges can impact the overall learning environment for a variety of reasons:

• Part-time faculty offer less variety in their instructional practices, are unavailable for extended student learning and advising, and are less connected with colleagues and the institution (Community College Survey of Student Engagement, 2012).

• Part-time faculty do not advise students as often, use active teaching techniques less often, spend less time preparing for class, and are less likely to participate in teaching workshops (Umbach, 2008).

• There is a negative impact on graduation rates at community colleges where higher percentages of part-time faculty are employed (Jacoby, 2006).

Recent research should, then, be interpreted by the part-time instructor as an important cautionary message. There are hurdles involved with teaching part-time that are recognized and must be addressed in order to help students succeed.

While an instructor may not be able to predict how students will react to their particular method of classroom facilitation; their attitude towards students and the conditions they create in the classroom will often determine if students continue their program. Student retention is not exclusively about numbers, it is the essence of interactions developed throughout the duration of the class. It all begins with the instructor.

## Student Engagement 101

As an instructor do you expect that your students will be active and present in the class? The level of a student's involvement in the class and the learning process are often assessed by his or her performance and the work product submitted; however, does active involvement equal engagement in the class? What does student engagement mean to you and to your class? Instructors must understand the process of engagement.

## Defining Student Engagement

Engagement is an action-based state that consists of the time, energy and effort which the student devotes to his or her class. The process of being engaged in the class involves more than the student just getting by in his or her class or doing the minimum required to pass the course. When students are engaged in a class, they are devoting the time necessary to become active participants in the process of learning and their attention is focused on the course.

A student may consciously think about being engaged in the class or it may occur as a reaction to specific requirements, such as a participation requirement or a group project. It is possible for the level of a student's engagement to frequently change, depending upon the interactions and experiences with other students and the instructor. For example, if the student is feeling confident with her/his progress and abilities, that positive emotion can enhance engagement. In contrast, if the student feels discouraged engagement and progress may diminish.

Adam Fletcher (2009) has found that "student engagement is increasingly seen as an indicator of successful classroom instruction."

Engagement may be enhanced or reduced if there is a feeling of being disconnected from the class or the instructor. Students who experience negative interactions may retreat from the class or withdraw their active engagement from the class as a reaction or retaliation for what they have experienced or how they have perceived a particular incident.

When adults experience engagement in what they are doing they are devoting their full attention to the task and they are enthusiastically involved, highly interested and experiencing positive emotions. Active engagement can lead to increased participation in the class discussions, which is a gauge that instructors often used to measure the level of a student's participation.

## The Instructor's Role in Student Engagement

The process of learning itself may produce emotional reactions that can influence engagement. If an instructor encourages students to utilize critical thinking and reflection, students are likely to experience a range of emotions while exploring their opinions, ideas and belief systems. The process of critical self-examination can happen while the student is working on his or her own or during classroom discussions, emphasizing the need for instructors to provide support and guidance. Instructors have the ability to establish classroom conditions which encourage positive interactions in a productive, respectful environment. When students feel positive emotions, and have experiences that produce positive emotions, they are likely to be fully engaged in the learning process and actively present in the class.

The instructor's level of engagement has a direct impact on a student's level of engagement. Students who believe their instructor is present in his or her class will be more active and engaged in the class as well. Students also react to their instructor's ongoing engagement in the class. The Maryville University website informs students that they will discover "enthusiastic professors with impressive academic credentials and professional experience." When instructors demonstrate a high level of enthusiasm as they engage in the class, it provides an example for students to follow.

Dr. Richard D. Jones (2008) notes that "it is easy to observe the lack of student engagement when students are slouched in their chairs and not listening to the teacher or participating in the discussion." From the instructor's perspective, adult learner engagement may be observed but not measured as the instructor is often focused on the required assignments, class discussions, and administrative aspects of classroom facilitation. In addition, many classroom assessments are designed to measure performance and progress towards meeting the required learning objectives rather than the level of engagement. Because student assessments are performance driven, engagement often becomes a criteria that is considered but not measured.

It is possible that increased engagement will have a positive impact on individual and classroom performance; therefore, instructors should consider methods of engaging students in the class.

## Encouraging Student Engagement

Factors which frequently influence student engagement in any classroom environment include family and career responsibilities. Other influences include attitude, prior class experiences, perceptions about the class, the instructor, and the ability of the course to meet students' needs. An instructor can take a pro-active approach and encourage student engagement through the following techniques.

Dr. Richard Jones (2008) reminds instructors that "relevance can help create conditions and motivation necessary for students to make the personal investment required for rigorous work or optimal learning," and that "students invest more of themselves, work harder, and learn better when the topic is interesting and connected to something that they already know."

Class discussions provide an opportunity to add relevance. An instructor can connect students to the course topics by sharing real world examples, experiences, and supplemental resources which bring the course topics to life.

Tristan de Frondeville (2009) notes that "although it may take years to develop the repertoire of skills and lessons that enable you to permanently create this active-learning environment, you can begin by discerning which activities truly engage your students." If a learning activity does not generate students' interest, then it is time to consider revising or eliminating that activity. While it is not possible to create excitement and enthusiasm for every class activity and assignment it is important to consider if the activities are busy work or something relevant to the learning objectives and have a potential to enhance the process of learning.

## Demonstrate Engagement for Your Students

It is possible to model active engagement in the class with daily participation postings, availability to address questions and concerns, and frequent communication.

Students who have negative interactions with their instructor or other students may retreat from the class or withdraw their active engagement from the class in retaliation for what they have experienced or how they have perceived a particular incident. As noted within the article "Drivers of Persistence" by the New England Literacy Resource Center, "it is human nature that when we feel welcomed, respected, and develop a sense of belonging, we are more apt to return to the setting or endeavor than when believes that instructors should "convey your passion and enthusiasm for the subject" and as a result "when students see their professor's passion, they want to participate." In a traditional classroom environment students physically observe their instructor's involvement in the class, along with their enthusiasm and passion. For the online classroom those characteristics are demonstrated through discussion boards and written communication.

## Other Factors Related to Student Engagement

Adam Fletcher (2009) has conducted a literature review of this topic and listed "five indicators for student engagement in college," which include "the level of academic challenge, active and collaborative learning, student-faculty interaction, enriching education experiences and a supportive learning environment." One method of addressing this list of indicators is to allow students to make choices concerning their assignments or involvement with the class as a means of encouraging them to feel that they had a choice in their level of engagement. For example, students could receive a list of possible topics for an assignment and choose one. Another method of connecting with students is to provide written feedback each week about the students' overall progress. Discuss specific resources that address their developmental needs.

Let's consider the questions posed in this chapter. Does active involvement equal engagement? If the students are actively involved in the class through their participation in discussions and the submission of assignments that demonstrate progress throughout the class, it is likely that instructors will view this level of involvement as engagement in the class.

What does student engagement mean to you and to your class? Instructors have the ability to influence student engagement in the class by providing support and guidance, being actively present in the class, developing meaningful interactions, and demonstrating engagement through their participation, passion, and enthusiasm. The goal is to create a learning environment that encourages students to be involved, because students who are highly motivated to participate in the learning process are likely to also be engaged.

**Bruce Johnson** *is an instructor of Communications at Cuyahoga Community College, Cleveland, OH.*

"In Their Own Words" essays are written by administrators, tenured and non-tenured faculty members who work at a variety of two- and four-year colleges and universities. We are grateful to these educators for sharing their insights and their expertise.

## Take a Break & Improve Student Attention

A study at the University of California at Berkeley has shown that college students only remember 20 percent of what they hear from a traditional lecture or demonstration several days after the class. Furthermore, this study also found that, in a room full of dozens of students, fewer than 15 percent are paying attention to what is being presented at any one time during the class, not counting the first eight minutes of a class when a much higher percentage of students are following the lecture.

The major reason for this is that students do not expend much energy thinking about what is being discussed in a traditional-style presentation. Students may also be so busy writing notes that they don't have the time to think about what they are actually doing.

It reminds me of a cartoon I have, showing a student returning home from school and telling his father, "They don't give us time to learn anything; we have to listen to the teacher all day." How very true. This does not mean that we should suddenly abandon lectures, but to make the best use of the time we have in a class to ensure students are actually learning. Otherwise, we might find that the following quote is all too true: "With the lecture, the information usually passes from the notes of the instructor to the notes of the students without passing through the minds of either!"

One thing that greatly influenced my own teaching when I became aware of the issue of student attention span was the book, *What's the Use of Lectures* book by Donald Bligh (1971). Not surprisingly the student level of attention is highest at the start of a lecture but begins to decline thereafter, and around 10-20 minutes into the lecture the level of attention begins to decrease dramatically and continues to decline for the rest of the hour until the last five minutes. In fact student attention has been shown to drop off after only 10 to 15 minutes. This suggests that the attention span of an average student might only be around 10-15 minutes during which time the most learning takes place.

Bligh notes that several studies have found a marked improvement in attention after a short break. The graph below shows the effect of a rest or change of activity on the level of attention after a break of a few minutes. If there is such a rest period, when the lecture resumes the amount of effective learning is almost as high as it was at the start of the lecture.

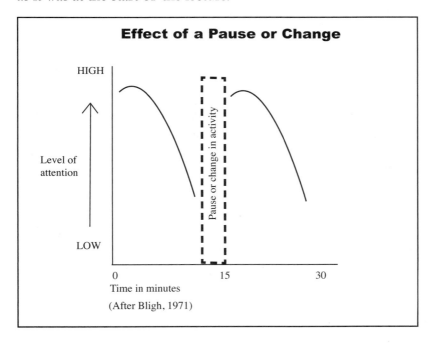

*Contributed by:* **Dr. Michael Collins** *author of* Teaching in the Sciences: A Handbook for Part-Time & Adjunct Faculty.

# TOPIC VII:

## Integrating Technology into the College Classroom: Current Practices and Future Opportunities

by Robin Lindbeck and Brian Fodrey

Faculty are integrating technology into the college classroom. But what are they doing? What's working? And how can we bring these ideas into other classrooms? As a result of questions like these the gap that currently exists between technology and effective teaching and learning strategies continues to widen (Lawless & Pellegrino, 2007). The integration of technology and proven pedagogy often suffers at the expense of each other. Yet, many studies conclude that faculty members continue to find ways to use technology that benefit both their fields of study and improving student learning.

### Instructional Strategies

Educators should sketch out a lesson plan that includes the instructional goals, objectives, and materials needed for the lesson and incorporate Gagne's nine events of instructions:

1. Gain attention – grab the learner's attention

2. Establish objectives – create an overview that explains the lesson and informs students of the objectives.

3. Stimulate prior recall – set the stage for the lesson.

4. Present lesson content – provide the lesson content with definitions and examples.

5. Provide learning guidance - give students opportunity to interact with the material with guidance and independently.

6. Elicit performance – utilize strategies that help students internalize the new skills and knowledge.

7. Provide feedback – allow for feedback and interpretation of the new information.

8. Assess performance – determine best ways to assess the students learning.

9. Enhance retention and transfer – develop ways for students to demonstrate that they can transfer their learning from this lesson to another situation. (Kruse, 2009)

## Technology and Learning

The impact technology has on learning often impacts the success of both the student and instructor. Consequently, attention may be paid to what teachers need to know in order to incorporate technology in the classroom…but little attention is paid to how. Mishra and Koehler (2006) introduced the "Technological Pedagogical Content Knowledge" (TPCK) framework that compensates for this lack of focus on the how, and "goes beyond merely identifying problems with current approaches" and instead "offers new ways of looking at and perceiving phenomena and offers information on which to base sound, pragmatic decision making" (p. 1019). TPCK which incorporates "Technology" as a third emphasis in Shulman's already widely popular "Pedagogical Content Knowledge" framework is described as:

… the basis of good teaching with technology and requires an understanding of the representation of concepts using technologies; pedagogical techniques that use technologies in constructive ways to teach content; knowledge of what makes concepts difficult or easy to learn and how technology can help redress some of the problems that students face; knowledge of students' prior knowledge and theories of epistemology; and knowledge of how technologies can be used to build on existing knowledge and to develop new epistemologies or strengthen old ones (Mishra & Koehler, 2006, p. 1029).

The manner in which identifying how technology can be interwoven into pedagogy and content reverses the already widely accepted practice of forcing each into an already selected (or pre-determined) technology, regardless of potential effectiveness.

In addition to re-examining how technology can be used to enhance learning, Selwyn (2007) states that little continues to be done in addressing the "limited, linear, and rigid terms" of how technology is currently being used in education. As a result, much of the innovation and creativity associated with developing successful instructional technology practices are often stifled by non-technological resistance and politics (Selwyn, 2007). Support and buy-in from faculty is also critical in ensuring that the role of technology continues to have a place in the effective classroom. Simply purchasing more technology will not increase effective use; instead a shift in confidence and strategy may be the most useful in fostering new and inventive technology integration practices (Surry & Land, 2000).

## Technology in Education

The impact technology has on education can be found at all levels, and with varying levels of success. Despite the obvious differences in student population, there are similarities that exist between higher education and K-12 schools regarding technology integration approaches. Hew and Brush (2007) describe barriers and strategies currently experienced in K-12 schools including overcoming lack of resources, developing a shared vision and plan for integration, as well as changing the attitudes, beliefs and ability levels of all those who use and learn with technology. These can be seen in higher education as well.

Therefore there is a need for a systematic strategy and evaluation of technology's role in education and faculty preparedness to best identify how to move forward in today's classroom (Lawless & Pellegrino, 2007). This includes efforts such as identifying how technology is currently being integrated in classrooms, what increases school and instructor adaptation, and defining long-term evaluation strategies. These are possible steps in assessing not only the state of educational technology, but also its promise (Lawless & Pellegrino, 2007). Because there is no one educational experience that will fulfill a student's need to use technology, nor technology-infused vision of teaching and learning for an instructor (Ertmer, Gopalakrishnan & Ross, 2001). The best course of action for successful technology integration is to provide:

… realistic visions of what others have achieved, teachers may be motivated to begin their own journeys toward exemplary technology use. Only by working within teachers' existing situations, can we truly expect best practice to be achieved (Ertmer, Gopalakrishnan & Ross, 2001).

## Collaboration Technologies

Although occasionally used in class, technologies used for collaboration are primarily supplements or extensions to the classroom experience. Some of these technologies are used as tools for students and faculty to have real-time, synchronous collaboration outside the typical classroom environment through real-time creation and editing of documents, as well as working together through videoconferencing such as Skype and chat. Most of these collaborative technologies, however, are used as asynchronous tools for collaboration. Using these tools students and faculty are able to share thoughts, ideas, and conversations back and forth through discussion boards, blogs, wikis, voicethreads, Twitter and email/voicemail. They are also able to use knowledge sharing tools like Delicious, Diigo, and hashtagging in other tools such as Twitter to identify, as they work the resources they find to be interesting and useful.

## Individual Technologies

Technologies in this category support student assignment and project work. Equipment such as computers, digital cameras and recorders, scanners, iPods and software such as mapping, inspiration, and image editing help students complete assignments or create projects for class and in some subject areas provided them with hands-on experience with the tools of the field. Other resources such as e-reserves and file exchange provide faculty and students with updated tools for handling the traditional tasks of reading packets and paper grading/returning. E-portfolios give students a structure to document their learning and skill development throughout their college experience, in addition to being able to easily share their work with future employers and colleagues.

Textbooks are increasingly accompanied by websites which provide supplementary content and exercises. Supporting websites include instructional materials such as movies, interactive exercises, Power-Point presentations and often an electronic version of the textbook. The instructor will need to review the contents of the website to determine the appropriate time to introduce its material in the curriculum. Homework assignments, supplementary content, diagnostic tests using multimedia sound and graphics are usually included on the websites. Exercises can be designed to give the student practice in discrimination, generalization, sequence and psychomotor learning. Each is defined as follows:

- **Discrimination** is the ability to differentiate between several items,

- **Generalization** is the ability to put like items in groups,

- **Sequencing** teaches how to get things done in the right order, and

- **Psychomotor learning** teaches skills using the hands by simulating the physical activity.

## Most Effective Technologies

The following list is drawn from research published by the National Social Science Association. A total of 106 faculty participated in a study about their use of technology in the classroom. The left hand column of the table, below, shows how many faculty indicated a particular technology was effective in the classroom. (Lindbeck and Fodrey, 2012).

| #faculty mentions | Type of Technology |
|---|---|
| 28 | Video |
| 23 | Powerpoint/Keynote/Slideshare |
| 19 | Internet (resource, music, photos) |
| 14 | Discussion board/Forum |
| 12 | Web 2.0 collaborative |
| 10 | Lecture capture / screen capture |
| 10 | MS Office/Google apps & docs |
| 10 | Video conferencing/ web conferencing |
| 9 | Blogs |
| 9 | Wiki |
| 8 | SmartBoard |
| 7 | Podcasts |
| 5 | Audience response system/Clickers |
| 5 | Video/computer projector |
| 4 | Second Life/Virtual world |
| 3 | Email/Voicemail |

*Printed with permission,* National Social Science Technology Journal, *El Cajon, CA.*

Roles change as students use technology as a tool or as a support for communicating with others. Instead of taking on a passive role of receiving information from the teacher, students take an active role in learning. The opportunity to work on authentic, meaningful, and challenging problems is provided when technology is used within the classroom. When students interact with data this promotes student-directed learning, and builds knowledge collaboratively. Teachers are given the opportunity to act as facilitators or guides. Students are enabled to solve real-world problems, retrieve information from online resources and connect with experts (Singh & Means, 2000).

A universally reported effect is the increase in motivation that occurs when students become involved with technology. Students with less initiative or facility with conventional academic tasks have shown a level of technology-based accomplishment. Some teachers report that there is a greater willingness to write or to work on computation skills. As Singh and Means (2000) state technology presents a very different set of challenges and different ways in which students can demonstrate their comprehension compared to conventional classroom settings with verbal knowledge or multiple-choice test performance.

Technologies can support the acquisition of basic skills but should be integrated carefully. The use of technologies can add value in allowing students to develop higher-order thinking skills. The can increase student motivation, improve teaching and learning, and help students reach higher levels of achievement.

**Robin Lindbeck** *is an assistant professor in the Organization Leadership & Performance Dept. at Idaho State University.*

**Brian Fodrey** *is Assistant Dean for Information Technology in the University of North Carolina School of Government.*

# TOPIC VIII:

## What is Critical Thinking?

### By Elizabeth T. Tice

Actually, that is a good question. The word *thinking* can describe any number of cognitive activities and there is certainly more than one way to think. However, critical thinking has become a highly debated topic in educational circles in recent years. Elementary school teachers to graduate school professors are advocating that critical thinking be integrated into all curricula. But what is critical thinking anyway? Who defines it?

Critical thinking often refers to mental activity that typically originates in the left hemisphere of the brain. But is critical thinking more than being logical? It is true that critical thinking requires analytical and logical reasoning and demonstrates higher level thinking skills. But it is more than that. Understanding logic appears to be a necessary condition to become a critical thinker, however, it is not a sufficient condition. It is my belief that, while critical thinking requires logical reasoning skills, the two are not synonymous. Logic itself is not critical thinking.

In order for teachers to incorporate critical thinking into their classrooms, they must understand what it is and is not. Therefore, in this topic section we will examine some of the current definitions and debates around critical thinking and how critical thinking can be viewed in the construct of cognitive development theory. We will also explore the relationship between thinking logically and thinking critically and the effect of emotion on critical thinking.

### Definitions of Critical Thinking

Ask ten people who believe themselves knowledgeable about critical thinking for a definition, and you will most likely receive ten differing responses. It seems that, although we have agreed upon the importance of critical thinking skills, we are struggling with the conceptual details.

Part of the problem may be that a dominant theoretical model of critical thinking does not yet exist. Definitions seem to vary by context (Tucker, 1997). As the Dean of the College of General Studies (and an instructor of critical thinking) at the University of Phoenix, I have endured many faculty debates on what we should actually teach in a Critical Thinking course.

Browne and Keeley (2014) refer to critical thinking as filtering— separating the relevant from the irrelevant. Chaffee (2014) says that critical thinking is "making sense of our world by carefully examining our thinking and the thinking of others in order to clarify and improve our understanding" (p. 49). Others (Missimer, 1990; Kahane, 2013; Beardsley, 1975; Freeman, 1993) define critical thinking much more technically: understanding argument, recognizing fallacies, distinguishing premises from conclusions, and isolating salient issues from irrelevant information.

Brookfield (2011) long considered an "expert" on critical thinking, contends that critical thinking is a process. Although his definition includes emotional as well as rational components, and clearly acknowledges the importance of culture and context, it contains the following common characteristics:

1. Identifying and challenging assumptions,
2. Challenging the importance of context,
3. Trying to imagine and explore alternatives, and
4. Reflective Skepticism (pp. 7-9).

Brookfield defines reflective skepticism as the act of constantly questioning the status quo. Just because something has been believed for years does not necessarily mean that it is true. Just because someone of perceived importance (like professors, for example) says something is right, that does not prove that it is right. I like to call this the "maybe—maybe not" life stance.

To all the above definitions, I say—yes. They all describe, to one extent or another, critical thinking. Actually the above definitions have many things in common, although the terminology might differ. The common threads throughout most writers' beliefs are (a) the importance of a good foundation in formal and informal logic, (b) the willingness to ask questions, and (c) the ability to see the relevant answers, even if they don't coincide with our pre-existing beliefs.

## Critical Thinking in the Construct of Cognitive Development

It is helpful to examine critical thinking through the construct of cognitive development theory. Many cognitive theorists believe that concrete logic is not possible until at least age 6 or 7, and that only in the highest levels of cognitive development can critical thinking take place. Jean Piaget, the noted psychologist and developmental theorist, postulates the following stages of development:

1. **Sensimotor Stage**: Birth to age 2 (approximately). Children begin with no thinking structures (called schema) and develop them through exploration of their senses and experimentation on the environment. Significant cognitive development occurs, but children in the sensorimotor stage are incapable of logical thought.

2. **Pre-Operational Stage**: Ages 2 to 7 (approximately). Children rapidly develop language skills and more sophisticated cognitive structures but are still pre-logical. They are not capable of conservation (the ability to understand that substance does not change although it changes shape or form). They are also incapable of de-centering (the ability to see things from another's perspective). Conservation and de-centering are prerequisite to logical thinking.

3. **Concrete Operational Stage**: Ages 7 to adolescence. Children begin to grasp conservation and de-centering. They begin to question: How does Santa really get to all those houses in one night? They can now reason logically but only on a concrete level, not hypothetically or abstractly. They solve problems logically but haphazardly.

4. **Formal Operations Stage**: Adolescence and above. The person is now capable of sophisticated logical thought. He or she can think in the abstract, can think hypothetically and can solve problems using the logic of combinations (Dworetzky & Davis, 1995).

Piaget's stages ended with Formal Operations, but Riegel (1973) has postulated a fifth stage called **Dialectical Reasoning**. This is a stage beyond logic where, I believe, real critical thinking lies. It is the ability to perceive the frequent paradoxes in life (to see the dialectic) and to question and analyze the assumptions that underlie the logic. Dialectical thinkers "readily recognize, accept, and even enjoy conflict and contradictions in values and possible courses of action because sorting out these conflicts forces them to grow intellectually" (Dworetzky & Davis, 1995, p. 360). A logical thinker can recognize and analyze the relationships between premises and conclusions. A critical thinker is able to extract and examine the assumptions that underlie the premises.

## The Relationship Between Logic and Critical Thinking

As stated earlier, logical reasoning seems to be a necessary, but not a sufficient condition for the development of critical thinking skills. It appears that one must be able to think logically, recognize fallacious reasoning, and construct valid arguments in order to think things through critically. However, one can understand the format of valid syllogisms, yet have no ability to understand cultural context or challenge assumptions. This seems to be at the core of most definitions of critical thinking. Skills in logical analysis provide the tools necessary to become a critical thinker.

In my Critical Thinking classes, I use the story of Jack and the Beanstalk to demonstrate the concept of challenging assumptions (an exercise shared with me by Toni LaMotta, a faculty colleague at the University of Phoenix). I ask students to relate the story and then ask them to name the hero of the story. Without hesitation, most of them name Jack. We then look at Jack's behavior in the story: he disobeyed his mother, he trespassed on the Giant's property, he stole the Giant's possessions, and he ultimately murdered the Giant. The compelling question here is—Who decided that Jack is a hero? The answer is that we did, culturally speaking. A critical thinker can see the underlying cultural assumptions in everyday happenings.

A critical thinker can understand that, although terrorism is abhorrent, it can be understood when viewed from the *cultural perspective* of the terrorist. A purely logical thinker will accept the following syllogism: Terrorism against the US is bad. The Islamic Jihad are terrorists against the US. Therefore the Islamic Jihad are bad. A critical thinker will not condone that act of terrorism, but will understand that there is more to the story than this simple, logically valid syllogism presents. He or she will understand that the Islamic Jihad are very similar to the early American revolutionaries; that they believe passionately in their cause; that in their culture this cause is all important; that the United States has manipulated their country for years, and that they could not possibly fight the United States on our terms. Saddam Hussein showed the world what happens to anyone who tries to fight the most powerful nation in the world in a conventional war. The early revolutionaries understood this and committed acts (such as the Boston Tea Party) that the British population living comfortably in England surely viewed as terrorism.

A critical thinker understands the cultural context of both examples and why Americans call the revolutionaries in our past *heroes*, yet call the Islamic revolutionaries *terrorists*.

## Emotionality and Critical Thinking

From a purely logical perspective, any emotion is illogical. In fact, *appeal to emotion* is one of the most common logical fallacies. Seech (2004) writes extensively about logical vulnerability. He defines logical vulnerability as the inability to be logical about a given issue because one is too emotionally invested in it.

However, in the transition from logical thinking to critical thinking, emotion and intuition must be re-introduced to the equation. The difference, I believe, lies in the thinker's ability to recognize the impact of emotion on logical thinking, and to choose the best alternative that allows for the importance of both logic and intuition. A critical thinker can believe passionately in his or her own religious belief system, yet still maintain a big picture understanding that it is not the *only acceptable* religious belief system.

Brookfield (2011) asserts that the journey to critical thinking often begins with a highly emotional "trigger event" (p. 26). These events often have the effect of jolting us out of our comfort zones, forcing us to explore new territory. Trigger events can be positive or negative, although most anecdotal literature supports growth from negative events.

However, positive trigger events can also propel one down the road to critical thinking. Here is where we as educators can make a difference. Formal higher education often promotes critical thinking as does exposure to individuals whose critical thinking skills are more fully developed than our own (Brookfield, 2011). Typically, a trigger propels us into a period of appraisal. We internally explore the nature of the new learning. Many times a person becomes uncomfortable with the dissonance (a natural response) and tends to minimize and deny the new learning (Brookfield, 2011).

According to Brookfield (2011), the period of appraisal is followed by a period of exploration. Having finally accepted that the discrepancy and dissonance are real, we set out to make sense of it. We explore new ways to think and view the world. This exploration leads to the awareness of alternative perspectives and, paradoxically, the understanding that the abundance of alternatives often signals the lack of any one right choice. This phase is, in my opinion, the most difficult for people to endure.

Eventually, those who endure the anxiety come to Brookfield's final phase of Integration. Integration can involve radical life changes or invisible internal cognitive life changes. But change occurs.

Perhaps the reason that we have struggled so with a single definition of critical thinking is that it cannot be narrowly contained. Perhaps the fact that it seems to vary by context does not indicate that we have been inconsistent in our definition process; perhaps a core element of critical thinking is that it does indeed vary by context. And maybe we should just accept that. Not everything can be neatly categorized in our comfortably distinct boxes. After all, an important characteristic of critical thinkers is the ability to tolerate ambiguity and to discern among several shades of gray.

**Elizabeth T. Tice** *is President and CEO of Ashford University, San Diego, CA.*

# TOPIC IX:

## The Syllabus and Lesson Plan

By Kay Stephan

The old cliché, "You never get a second chance to make a good first impression" is especially true for the syllabus. The syllabus can give students the impression that you are organized and know the subject matter as well as how to present it; or it can give the impression that you are disorganized and do not know how to run a class. Just as in other situations, the first impression may or may not be true; however, most would prefer making that first impression in a classroom a favorable one.

The syllabus provides your students with a roadmap of what the course will cover and what is expected of them. It will cover policies and provide information necessary for the successful completion of the course. In addition to providing directions, the syllabus should also be thought of as a contract between you and your students. Students know what they need to do to earn the desired grade, including readings, term papers, quizzes, tests and other activities. A good syllabus will also provide policies such as "make-up" work and attendance. Take the advice of experienced teachers: the time and care taken to build a good syllabus will reap many benefits the entire term. The carefully written syllabus will protect you and your college when students try to alter the rules or challenge grades. If students see policies up front, there should be relatively few questions that can later cause problems. For instance if there is a request for a make-up exam, you should be able to refer to your syllabus and answer the question in a way that is fair to all students, not just the one requesting the make-up exam.

At first glance it could appear that this detailed syllabus is restrictive to your academic freedom. However, it's better to think of it as a guide and even a checklist that provides details of course requirements and college policies that could prevent misunderstandings and grievance procedures as well as providing students with a prescription for success. The outline that is described below can be thought of as a skeleton. An instructor is free to add information and put the syllabus in any format that is clear, readable, and reproducible.

In order to manage the numerous syllabus components, the syllabus will be split into three sections: the general course and instructor information, specific course requirements, and college policies.

## General Course and Instructor Information

These components are basic, require little explanation, and are usually placed at the beginning of the syllabus. The parts are as follows:

- **Course Title**
- **Course Number**
- **Number of credit hours**
- **Class meeting days and times**
- **Term name and year**
- **Course description and prerequisites**
- **Instructor's name and title**
- **Instructor's office telephone number**
- **Instructor's office hours**
- **Instructor's home or cell phone number** (Optional)
- **Instructor's email address**
- **Instructor's website**

## Specific Course Requirements

These components explain specifically what the course is and what is expected of each student. This is the most crucial section and provides the most salient information. Any logical order of the components is acceptable.

- Be sure to list all **required materials**, including author(s), title, and edition of the textbook(s). You should also include all supplies, equipment and/or other special needs. It is difficult to require a student to purchase an expensive calculator in the middle of the semester, especially if the "drop class" period has passed. You need to determine all materials necessary, not covered by some type of course fee, that the student must purchase.

- One of the hardest things for many adjuncts to write is the **course rationale**. This explains how the course fits into the student's curriculum as well as why the course is of value in and of itself. You could ask a coordinator or department head about curriculum matters and if the course is a degree requirement. However, it is a good process for you, as the instructor, to think about the value or rationale for the course. This process can provide you with insight and direction for preparing your curriculum. (If you cannot verbalize the value of the course, then what do you think your students will find valuable about it?)

- A good syllabus will provide **course learning outcomes**. Your college may already have basic outcomes for each course in the curriculum. Again, check with your coordinator or department head to be sure that all minimum standards are met. Naturally, you may wish to add an outcome or two, but the basic ones should be consistent across all course sections. These outcomes should not be just words on a paper, but rather a guide that provides direction on what needs to be covered and mastered within the course. Since these outcomes are the backbone of your course, consider them carefully and determine how each will be measured.

- Some college administrations recommend **a statement about assessment**. Since most college instructors are now required to be very attentive to assessment activities, students should also know what assessment is, why it is important, what activities will be included in the course, and what, if any, activities will be considered a part of the grade. (In my class I have an ungraded pre-test, and the graded comprehensive final exam is considered the post-test. However, some instructors use a series of ungraded activities. Whatever you plan, students need to know how assessment activities will be used.)

≈ You need to carefully decide all the **course requirements** before preparing your syllabus. Since the syllabus is considered a contract, you cannot add requirements halfway through the term. The requirements may include quizzes, tests, papers, journalizing, readings, portfolios, etc. You could even include attendance as part of the requirements. Just be sure to include everything the students need to successfully complete the course.

≈ The syllabus should also include a **brief statement of the instructional methods** you will use. Examples of these include but are not limited to lecture, group work, films, guest speakers, panel discussions, and question-and-answer drills. Providing instructional methods will give students a preview of the class and what could be expected to happen during class sessions.

≈ Perhaps the most tedious task of preparing the syllabus is providing **a content outline for the entire course**; however, once designed, it will provide an excellent guide for daily class preparation for you as the instructor as well as for your students. This section should include a tentative outline of class topics and critical dates such as assignment due dates, tentative exam dates, holiday(s), and/or days when the class will not meet.

≈ At the heart of an good syllabus is **the section on grading**

**strategies and criteria**. Students need to know how their final grade will be computed. For example, four tests may be worth 100 points each for a maximum of 400 points of the 1000 points possible, or the average of any number of tests may count as 40% of the grade. No matter how you set up your grading system, be sure to provide a grading scale and percentage weights of all components of the final grade. Include how the percentage grades will be converted into a letter grade, i.e. 94% earns an "A" while 93% earns an "A-." (If your school has a required grading scale, it would be in the college catalog.) Your grading criteria should include policies for accepting and/or evaluating assignments submitted after due dates, make-up test policies, etc. You may require that all work be turned in the day the student returns to class after an absence. It could be that quizzes cannot be made up and the lowest grade is dropped. You could also require a student to call you if they are going to miss a test. If the student does not follow the policy, then the test cannot be made up. Whatever you decide, be sure to express policies clearly on the syllabus and orally point them out during the first day of class. Not providing a concrete policy for make-up work can become a crux of controversy involving you, your students and the administration.

~ If you have an **attendance policy**, include it in your syllabus with clear instructions on how attendance counts in the final grade. Check the college catalog to see if there is a college-wide attendance policy. (An effective policy that I put in all my syllabi is that the student gets 10 bonus points for missing no more than one class for any reason.)

## College Policies

This last section deals with policies that the college has developed for all students. This information is basically boilerplate and will be available electonically. These policies may include the following:

- **Registration Policy** – This has to do with students on the college's official class lists and when students may no longer attend classes if their names do not appear on the list.

- **Students with Disabilities Policy**

- **Inclement Weather Policy**

- **Withdrawal Policy**

- **Fees and Refund Schedules**

- **Term Calendar** – This would list when classes begin, when the college is closed, final refund dates, last day to drop and add classes and the final examination period.

Once you have completed your course syllabus, you are well on your way to planning an effective course. **Some authorities feel that the syllabus is the most important document in academia since it defines the course and all requirements.** Yes, it takes a great deal of time to design a good syllabus; but like most things involved with teaching, the first time is the most difficult. After all, you can make minor adjustments as necessary to refine the original syllabus. Also, once you have major policies worked out, many can be transferred from course to course. Take the time necessary to plan your syllabus. It will be worth it and will certainly make that first impression a good one.

## The Lesson Plan

The lesson plan is a "must do" for effective teaching. If you have a well-designed course outline, the daily lesson plan is much easier to prepare. These are numerous formats for lesson plans; you need to select one that works for you. (Some teachers use a loose-leaf notebook to keep lesson plans and notes; others use one file folder for each lesson and even color codes for different classes.) While the syllabus is fairly cut and dry, the lesson plan can reflect your creative side. It can reflect your personality and teaching style as long as it directs effective learning.

Before you start to plan the lesson, you need to determine the day's objectives. These are the focal point of any plan. You must know what you need to teach, and you must be able to verbalize it to your students. There can be a variety of ways of attaining the objectives, but you first need to decide what they are.

After determining your objectives, then outline the major topics you will cover, including definitions and reference to sources that are not included in the textbook. With computer slide presentations available with many textbooks, the chapter outlines may already be prepared. (I print the outlines and then add my supplementary notes. For long or difficult concepts, I may even print the outline for students. Doing this allows them to focus on the lesson instead of taking copious notes.)

Next you will need to determine how you will get the major points across to students. Lecturing, of course, is one way; but it may not always be the most effective strategy. This is where your creativity and imagination come into play. Adding personal anecdotes and experiences help bring a lesson to life. You should also try to stimulate active student participation. Generally students will retain knowledge much longer if they actively participate in the classroom activity.

Any experienced teacher can recall classroom episodes where things did not go as planned. Equipment didn't work, an activity fell flat, or students did not understand the lecture. That is why the best lesson plan allows for flexibility, and the best teachers can adjust to unpredictable experiences and audiences. But no matter what happens, if the lesson objectives are identified, the teacher can adjust his or her teaching approach and still meet the objectives.

Your lesson plan should include everything you need to take to the classroom such as notes, handouts, or computer disks. It should also include instructor and student activities and homework assignments with due dates.

In many of my classes I have adopted the practice of preparing a weekly agenda for each student. The agenda includes daily objectives, what chapters will be covered and the homework assignments with due dates. Students appreciate having this written documentation in order to plan their busy week in advance. I also have a file folder in the classroom where student know they can pick up the agenda if they have missed a class.

Planning is the job of all good teachers. Whether it is the syllabus or the daily lesson plan, you must spend the time necessary to plan effective learning strategies. You should also make notes on the lesson plans to remind yourself of what activities worked well and which ones need to be modified. Keeping a careful record of your lessons will make teaching easier from year to year. You will also develop a portfolio of ideas and activities that you can use in many teaching situations. Take the time and plan!

**Kay Stephan** *is owner and founder of Classic Protocol, Inc. She has over 25 years experience as a teacher, business coach and recognized advocate for office professionals. She served for many years as Director of Adjunct Faculty for the University of Akron at Wayne College, Orrville, OH.*

# TOPIC X:

## Motivating the Student in the College Classroom

By Hikmat Chedid

Delivering a well-prepared lecture is just one of the necessary conditions for achieving success in today's classrooms. A successful instructor realizes that achieving success requires ensuring that students, and specifically the less attentive students, are motivated to comprehend and retain the material. The literature clearly reflects that motivation is essential to achieving excellence in the classroom. The following are methods I use in my classroom to engage the less motivated.

### ✌ Deliver the first couple of lectures from the back of the classroom.

I began to notice over the years that less motivated students fill the seats that are farthest away from the instructor's desk. Those students, whom I get to know better later in the semester, tend to be less motivated but sometimes only shy and want to keep to themselves. I deliver my first lecture and some subsequent lectures from the back of the room, making clear but not aggressive eye contact with the students. These are attempts to confirm to them that they are important to me, and that they deserve and will be accorded personal attention. I think of it as a personal invitation to each of them to become an active participant in the classroom. Often students accept this invitation, and it turns out to be all that is required to motivate a particular student to become active and to take ownership of his learning.

**෫ Assign extra credit points for class participation.**

I assure students that I will not call on them to answer
questions unless they indicate their willingness to answer
the question by raising their hands. I assign a healthy
number of extra credit points toward class participation,
and remind students often of their many predecessors
who achieved a higher grade as a result of those extra
credit points. I am always surprised to find that those
points motivate even the most shy students and convince
them to participate regularly in classroom discussions.
However it is imperative to compliment students on the
quality of their questions: "Good question, Mr. Reeves, I
am glad you asked about that…" "Excellent answer! Ms.
Johnson…."

**෫ Ask students to express their goals for the course,
and relate the course material to those goals.**

I ask each student to introduce himself or herself during
the first class, and to explain his or her reason for taking
the course. From the students' comments, I synthesize
several class goals. Subsequently, I begin my lectures by
explaining how the material being presented relates to the
long-term goals of the students. It is critical to explain to
students, preferably through real examples, why they are
learning a particular concept and how they will encounter
the concept on the job.

**෫ Be enthusiastic about the subject matter, and show
your enthusiasm.**

Enthusiasm is contagious; an enthusiastic teacher thinks
of unusual real-life examples to relate the concept. I let
not only my body language—teaching on my feet, using
good eye contact, standing close to the students, using a
lively tone of voice (although sometimes I run the real

risk of loosing my voice), and radiating a positive overall demeanor—demonstrate a professional image and show my enthusiasm, but I truly have fun with the subject. I find myself acting out concepts, confronting common misconceptions, and presenting intuitive results. Have genuine fun in the classroom.

### ❧ Have high but compassionate standards.

High and positive expectations usually produce excellent and positive outcomes. Let me define the two terms. Most know what is meant by the term "high standard". If you guessed that it meant difficult exams and homework assignments that require a great time commitment, you are correct. "Compassionate" refers to a realization on the professor's part that some college students are not the traditional full-time "just out of high school" students. These students might be single parents or individuals holding two jobs. While the course outcomes must not be reduced to allow students to pass undeservedly, the professor must be willing to extend the student extra help on an one-on-one basis, and at times and hours that might not be ideal. I find that if students realize the applicability of a long and difficult project to their objective, and if they know their professor is genuinely willing to help them, they will rise to the occasion and become motivated to achieving success.

### ❧ Provide a class structure that allows students to make mistakes, learn from their mistakes, and try again with little or no punitive measures.

I allow students a chance to re-do and re-submit their exams for a higher grade. Not necessarily a full grade, but certainly an improved grade. I also explain to them that the same concept will appear on subsequent quizzes and examinations, particularly on the final exam. Those who learn from their current mistakes will avoid making them on a future quiz and as a result will earn higher grades. This method motivates students to research questions they missed, learn from their mistakes, and achieve better mastery of the course concepts.

### ❧ Administer quizzes frequently, to motivate students to do assignments regularly.

I ask students toward the beginning of the course to take a positive outlook on quizzes, and think of them as previews for the larger, more important examination. I encourage students to think of quizzes as a service to help them monitor their progress. Weekly quizzes motivate the student to do assignments regularly, uncover their problem areas, and make attempts to understand the concepts before the class is too far along. It is often required that the instructor hold one-on-one conferences with students who perform poorly on more than one quiz, but make no obvious attempt to improve.

### ❧ Create group activities to provide immediate experience with the concepts.

Performance-based group activities reinforce and lend clarity to difficult concepts. Students often do not realize that they do not understand a certain concept until they attempt to apply the concept to case studies or to formulate a solution to a real problem. Group performance-based activities uncover those deficiencies, and provide students an opportunity to measure their learning. Often these group activities are the first opportunity a student has to learn to work successfully with a difficult person, to learn attributes that lead to a successful team dynamic, and to become a successful team member. When conflicts occur between team members, as tempting as it is to step in and resolve the matter, I refrain from doing so to avoid robbing students of the opportunity to resolve the problem on their own, and to feel proud as a result of their experience.

ᵔ **Test fairly.**

Unfair examinations can discourage the best of students. However, testing fairly does not mean giving easy exams. To the contrary, one can give difficult but fair examinations. By exam time, students should be clear on the test objectives. The exam should be limited to those objectives. Difficult questions are encouraged as long as they are carefully examined after the exam is graded. Those questions missed by the majority of the students, should be factored out of the grade, evaluated for value added, explained to the class, and re-addressed in future quizzes and exams.

Achieving success in the classroom is directly correlated with the level of student motivation. Student motivation is a deliberate series of actions that can and should be designed into the course by the faculty member. One might argue that certain students come to the classroom with excellent motivation and do not require additional effort by the instructor. However, motivating those students who lack motivation is where the challenges and the rewards exist.

**Hikmat Chedid** *is professor of Engineering and Director of The Digital Forensics Institute at Lorain County Community College, Elyria, OH.*

# TOPIC XI:

## Collaborative/Cooperative Learning

By Arlene Sego

"What's the difference between collaborative and cooperative learning?" The terms collaborative learning and cooperative learning sometimes are used interchangeably. This is reasonable, as both favor small-group active student participation over passive, lecture-based teaching and each require a specific task to be completed. Each strategy inherently supports a discovery based approach to learning. The two methods assign various group roles though collaborative learning can have fewer roles assigned. In both situations, student members are required to possess group skills though cooperative learning may include this as a instructional goal. Each plan comes with a framework upon which the group's activity resides, but cooperative learning is usually more structurally defined than collaborative learning (Cooper and Robinson, 1998; Smith and MacGregor, 1992; Rockwood, 1995a, 1995b).

However, practioners point out that these two terms are different. Rockwood (Rockwood, 1995a, 1995b) characterizes the differences between these methodologies as one of knowledge and power: Cooperative learning is the methodology of choice for foundational knowledge (i.e., traditional knowledge) while collaborative learning is connected to the social constructionist's view that knowledge is a social construct. He further distinguishes these approaches by the instructor's role: In cooperative learning the instructor is the center of authority in the class, with group tasks usually more closed-ended and often having specific answers. In contrast, in collaborative learning the instructor abdicates his or her authority and empowers the small groups who are often given more open-ended, complex tasks. Rockwood uses both approaches depending on the academic maturity of his students. He favors the more structured cooperative learning style for foundational knowledge typified in gateway courses, and depends on the laissez faire approach of collaborative learning for higher level, less foundational knowledge content. Other terms are used as well in conjunction with collaborative/cooperative learning. These include: team learning; problem-based learning including guided design, case studies, simulations; peer-assisted instruction including supplemental instruction, writing fellows, mathematics workshops; discussion groups and seminars; learning communities; and lab work. Check the bibliography for more information about these.(Cooper and Robinson, 1998; MacGregor, 1990; Smith and MacGregor, 1992).

Collaborative learning is one of the oldest educational techniques, dating back to one-room schoolhouses where several grades were grouped together. In theory, collaborative learning brings students of differing abilities together in small groups where they teach each other the concepts of the formal class by reinforcing lecture and text materials. In practice, student groups either work on assigned projects cooperatively or take selected quizzes and/or tests together. The process forced all students to become actively involved in classroom activities. Even passive students are more inclined to become active when their participation is required for the ultimate success of their partners. Adult learners relate to collaboration in the classroom because of the similarity to the cooperation required in most contemporary workplaces.

College classrooms tend to have a more heterogeneous student base than those found in lower grades. But there are subtle differences between types of classes. Students in technical education classes are highly motivated, regardless of the specific academic skills they possess. Students in developmental classes generally will be hampered by the fact that they have fewer basic English and mathematics skills with which to solve problems. Traditional academic classes, however, will be a composite of students' abilities, purpose, and motivation. But no matter the type of class or teaching method, virtually all academic and technical disciplines can benefit from the inclusion of collaborative techniques in the classroom.

For instructors there are two basic prerequisites for collaborative learning: thorough planning and a *total* commitment. As a facilitator, the instructor becomes an idea person, a resource person, a mediator (conflict resolution is as much of an accomplishment in collaborative education as it is in the workplace or in life itself) and a supporter of the students' efforts.

Preliminary planning by faculty for collaborative classroom activities includes the determination of classroom goals, specific activities that can be assigned cooperatively, and the balance sought with traditional teaching methods. Ideally a collaborative activity should be started the first week of class. If grades are going to be assigned for group work, the students must be made aware of this at the beginning of the term; the assignment of the same grade to each member of a group is the incentive needed to make collaboration work effectively. Adult learners are always concerned about how they will be graded in a class, so students should be informed what part of the final grade will be the result of the collaborative efforts.

The optimum size for a work group is four or five students, especially if the students are working on a project or other activity that will be graded. More than five students can be unwieldy while fewer than four opens the door to domineering students. Groups can be formed by:

- students themselves,
- the instructor assigning students to groups,
- random assignment, or
- selection based upon similar interests or specific criteria.

However, decided disadvantages accompany student-based selection. Students often choose to be with friends (which excludes assimilation of new students into the mainstream of the class) and there may be stress in arranging groups if students do not know each other and have no basis for selection.

Some collaborative experiences will lend themselves to completion during one class period while others will take days or even weeks to complete. Overlapping activities will add to the cohesiveness of the group structure. Giving students the opportunity to talk with each other begins the interaction that is one of the important components for success in collaborative learning.

Not all collaborative activities need to be structured or grade-based. Students will respond to a change in classroom pace when they have the opportunity to react with partners. Group work can be used to reaffirm techniques that have been presented, analyze material from differing perspectives, or brainstorm for solutions to problems presented by the instructor. Let students know what is expected from them during their impromptu activity so it does not become a social event.

Although it is important to give explicit instructions about the nature and purpose of a collaborative activity plus how groups are to operate, leave students latitude for their own group innovations. The instructor is the facilitator for activities. Students are the active participants. Provide a classroom atmosphere whereby students feel free to contribute creative ideas without fear of criticism.

When students are able to physically move chairs together for group activities they can focus on each other, rather than the teacher. If a classroom has tables and chairs or desks permanently attached to the floor, allow students to move so that they are in close proximity to each other. Groups inherently try to physically move away from other groups of students. Interestingly, collaboration invariably brings a louder than usual level and excitement to the classrooms, but students are so engrossed helping each other they tend to ignore the other groups.

Adults can be sensitive to how others view them and tend to be more candid when working in small groups; working with fellow students provides adults the opportunity to explore new horizons in their subject area.

The benefits of collaborative learning include:

- ❧ Adults have a vehicle **to get to know others** in class,
- ❧ **Attendance tends to be better** (a result of a commitment to the group),
- ❧ **Improved grades** due to increased understanding of the subject matter,
- ❧ Classroom groups **foster study groups** outside of the class, and

   *~* Students **become active participants** in their own
    learning.

Teachers regularly must re-evaluate their classroom styles to accommodate changes in technology, student abilities and student demands. Collaborative learning is but one of many viable strategies to encourage participation by students. Obstacles that might be encountered are: some students may feel they paid money to take the course, therefore the teacher should stand in front of the class and lecture; groups may not take an assignment seriously; and some individuals may have difficulty working within a group. However, problems can be overcome by involving students in decisions regarding the progression of collaborative activities.

Many colleges now provide students with the opportunity to achieve educational goals outside the traditional classroom setting by the use of hybrid, online and blended courses. At first glance there is a perception that students will only learn facts, without the opportunity to develop critical thinking skills. But interaction between students and with the faculty member can be achieved through the use of email, chat groups and listservs. More progressive institutions of higher learning already provide campus email for adjunct faculty, so it is worthwhile to find out what is available. Be aware, however, that at many institutions an adjunct faculty member's campus email account may be deleted at the end of each semester.

No one method of teaching can ever be an end unto itself. The use of collaborative learning is but one of many viable classroom strategies to encourage the participation of your students. But with its use, adult students tend to be more comfortable in an academic setting, which translates into improved subject matter skills and the desire to continue their education.

**Arlene Sego** *served as an adjunct faculty mentor/trainer. She is the author of several publications on cooperative/collaborative learning.*

"In Their Own Words" essays are written by administrators, tenured and non-tenured faculty members who work at a variety of two- and four-year colleges and universities. We are grateful to these educators for sharing their insights and their expertise.

## Applications of Cooperative Learning in the Classroom

Cooperative learning processes may be used in a variety of ways across the curriculum to help groups to develop critical thinking skills, to remain task oriented and accountable, and to benefit from the findings of the subgroups.

### Cooperative Learning Communities

Synergy results when students cooperate in the learning process. Students are aware of the synergy in their daily lives. They know that when a group gathers for a common purpose, the energy in the group and the capability of the group creates a stronger, more compelling response than that generated by one person working alone. Additionally, when group members make their own decisions regarding details of a proposed learning outcome, they become stakeholders in the process. Collaborative decision making reflects the effectiveness of the learning community brought together mutually to learn and to share together.

At the beginning of the course, the instructor (as facilitator) may want to clarify how group processes work effectively. Groups should be encouraged to brainstorm without "shooting down" anyone's ideas, to maintain respect for each individual's contribution, to stay on the task, to participate actively, to honor time limitations and to set aside personal agendas.

Pairing or grouping students in dyads has the advantage of heightening accountability. When students learn in pairs, both present the results of their learning to the large group. For example, if each dyad is given a specific question, one student may verbalize the question and answer while the other student substantiates the answer.

In cooperative learning groups of three to five (more than five students in a group may not be as productive), the instructor may want to explain to students the task-oriented and maintenance-oriented functions of group members.

Task-oriented functions include those of initiating, seeking information, giving information, clarifying, summarizing and creating consensus. Maintenance-oriented functions include encouraging, gate keeping (awareness of distribution of time among group members), setting standards, harmonizing, relieving tension, expressing group feeling.

In a typical group experience, students may be asked to check the appropriate functions as they contribute to the group. Using a checklist may heighten awareness of the cooperative learning process.

## Types of Group Process

- **Dividing the Task:** In dividing the task, the instructor assigns part of a larger learning project to each group. Students divide their portion of the project into individual parts. Each student presents the individual findings to the group, which then synthesizes the individual responses into one answer that is shared with the class verbally and visually.

- **Critical Thinking Process:** Each group generates responses to the task together. This is especially beneficial when the objective of the task involves critical thinking questions. Group discussions of this type touch on a variety of answers and examine implications which otherwise might be overlooked. The quality of the responses is more thoughtful through group exchange. As each group presents the rationale for their findings verbally and visually, class discussion illuminates the results.

- **Multiple Options:** When each student is provided with an option of three or four questions on which to write or respond, students may be grouped according to their first preference. Each group then has the same clear goal in which each student is a stakeholder. Sometimes, as an additional option, it may be useful for students to subdivide the material. After each student has been given sufficient time to generate a thoughtful response, students share answers within the group.

- **Student Choice:** Students are offered various aspects of a question to explore. In their group, they decide their first and second choices and write these on the board. The class looks at the preferences of each group and decides together how to divide the material.

## Reporting Methods

When feasible, large group reporting methods are enhanced when, in addition to an oral report, a visual component is provided. Using an overhead transparency to elucidate how and when an answer was found (especially helpful in providing concrete evidence in problem solving) has the advantage of using both audio and visual learning styles, and students, working together, share accountability.

In small groups, the visual component may be provided as group members take notes on each report. Creative extensions may be provided by students with special talents through videos, slides, etc.

When students are part of the decision-making process and when collaborative/cooperative processes are used, group synergy, critical thinking skills, and success grow, leading students to a heightened awareness of their own untapped potential and empower.

*Contributed by:* **Eileen Teare** *of Lorain County Community College, Elyria, OH.*

# TOPIC XII:

## Student Learning Styles: Teaching Techniques for Student Success

By Michael Parsons

## Learning Paradigm Shifts

For the past decade a number of educational researchers have ex-amined the characteristics of student learning in order to improve student success and student retention. Previously it was assumed that students learned effectively by reading textbooks, listening carefully to synthesizing lectures, and applying deductive logic to examinations. Such well-known education researchers as Will McKeachie (University of Michigan), Howard Gardner (Harvard), and Pat Cross (University of California-Berkeley) now document that students learn best when they are involved directly with the materials they are to learn.

A number of strategies improve student ownership of learning. Focused discussion is a popular model. Cooperative learning uses teams of students to address problem solving and application skills. Technology including text, audio, video, animation and graphics, as well as the Internet provide the students with both input and control over the material being learned. All of these techniques require varying degrees of access to technology or the commitment of large blocks of instructional time.

While effective, they tend to lack both spontaneity and efficiency. There is a design for instruction that is as effective as those afore-mentioned, supports spontaneity, and can be tailored effectively to fit a variety of time and teaching frames.

### The Nominal Group Technique

In 1968 two social psychologists, Andre L. Debecq and Andrew Van de Ven designed a strategy called the Nominal Group Technique (NGT). It can be used to turn a heterogeneous class into a structured group for decision making. It may be applied in a variety of classes. Data provided by the instructor allows the students to engage in analysis, synthesis and evaluation activities. These higher order thinking skills enhance student knowledge and put the student in control of his or her learning. The process has four steps:

1.   **The data are provided to the students**. Each student is then asked to react individually by comparing his or her attitude, value or demographic base to the general summary.

2.   **A round-robin discussion** allows all members of the class to react to diverse responses.

3.   **A summary of class responses** is prepared which then becomes a micro-dataset to be compared with the larger one that initiated the activity.

4.   **An analysis of the differences** between the class information and the larger dataset and **an evaluation of the potential causes** for any disparity complete the activity.

The foregoing description is somewhat abstract; let's consider each component of the activity to better understand how this technique can be applied in a variety of classroom settings.

## Sources of Data

The NGT technique is particularly effective in social and behavioral science courses. A variety of federal and state organizations provide useful data summaries. I have used taxonomies of values derived from U.S. Department of Labor studies, prestige rankings of professions released by the U.S. Department of Interior, rankings of priorities for educational reform by U.S. Department of Education researchers, and rankings of student behavior drawn from studies produced by the American Council on Education. The information is available on the Internet, in daily newspapers (especially *USA Today*), and in weekly news magazines like *Time* and *U.S. News and World Report*. In each instance, individual student rankings and their class averages differed form the national databases. Student reactions to the strategy indicate that they are very interested in how they compare to other groups in society and are very willing to both analyze and evaluate the nature and causes of the divergence.

## NGT Organizational Design

The following steps can be used to implement an NGT activity:

1. **Present a set of data to the students, preferably in writing.** Explain to them that they are to read the questions or statements, disregard the ranking provided with the data and list their personal responses.

2. **The size of the dataset will determine the amount of time given to individual ranking.** I endeavor to use datasets that do not exceed two dozen questions or responses. The amount of time it takes for individual responses usually does not exceed 7-10 minutes.

3. Once the students are finished with individual rankings, **a general discussion is held of the types of responses elicited from the class.** The purpose of the round-robin is to enhance the student feeling of participation and ownership of the material.

4. Following the discussion, **students and the instructor construct a class response summary.** If the dataset is long, the instructor may choose to prepare the summary outside of class.

5. Using the summary as a guide, the instructor facilitates **an analysis of the similarities and dif-**

**ferences between the class summary and the dataset**. Students expand their personal ownership as well as begin the process of the class becoming a group in the sociological sense.

6.  The final step in the process is a synthesis. The students, guided by the faculty member, **evaluate the degree of congruence between course theory and the real world application** reflected throughout the dataset.

This activity adds a dimension of reality to course theory as well as assisting students in understanding how their classroom learning can be applied in the real world. Comments like "this is the first time I have ever understood what to do with course material" are not uncommon.

## Questions Frequently Asked About NGT

**☙ How many people can participate?**
In general, nominal groups are best with membership of approximately 8 to 10. It is relatively easy to divide a class of 30 into three of these groups. The faculty member as facilitator can move comfortably from one to another during the process of constructing a class response summary. Also, discussion can be class wide or in subsets. The strategy had a great deal of flexibility, depending upon classroom climate and instructor flexibility.

**☙ What characterizes a good dataset?**
Research into student learning styles reports that students bring with them attitudes, feelings, and mental models that impact on teaching/learning. Any dataset that allows students to compare their generic perceptions with those that are attitude- or values-based and short enough that they do not require class periods for application and analysis.

### ❧ What skills are required of students to use the technique?

In general, it is best to not use a technique like NGT until the class has begun to develop a sense of identity. The process is effective to the extent that the students are willing to share with each other and communicate relatively openly about values- and attitudes-based material. In general, I do not use these techniques until approximately one month into the semester or term. If a class is reticent to participate verbally, I would recommend simpler skill-building initiatives prior to using something as complex as NGT.

### ❧ What skills should the faculty member/facilitator possess?

The facilitator must have a comfort level with a variety of communication skills but most specifically listening and synthesizing. During both the discussion phase and summary-building phase, the facilitator must hear what the students are saying and, if uncertain, synthesize the responses as a way of seeking agreement. Also, the individual must have established a rapport with the class so that the students are willing to share and discuss emotionally charged material. Finally, the facilitator must be able to articulate the purpose of the exercise within the context of the purpose of the course. If the students do not feel "connected," their participation will be superficial.

### ❧ Are there disadvantages to NGT? When shouldn't it be used?

NGT is designed to foster higher order thinking, problem solving, and evaluation. It requires careful planning and a focused application. If the goal of the course is to simply encourage student presentation of material or student-to-student discussion, there are other less complex strategies that should be used.

## Why Do It?

All students expect more of their educations. We need to support them as they develop critical-thinking skills, problem-solving strategies and risk taking. Further, both students and employers are critical of education for not making students "work ready." NGT addresses all of these skills. If we are to be successful in preparing our clients for a rapidly changing world, we must "rethink our way."

**Dr. Michael Parsons** *was the Dean of Instruction at Hagerstown Community College in Hagerstown, MD from 1972-2000, and a Professor of Professor of Education and Social Science until 2011, when he retired. He is now an adjunct at Morgan State University.*

# TOPIC XIII:

## Teaching Students to Solve Problems

### By Sheri Bidwell

One important way that instructors can prepare students for success
in the workplace is to give them opportunities to learn and practice
problem-solving skills. Problem solving has been identified as one
of several critical workplace skills.

These and other skills, which were identified by the U.S. Secretary
of Labor's Commission on Achieving Necessary Skills (SCANS),
are listed below. The skills were identified and verified by a broad
range of employers representative of business, industry, labor, and
community-based organizations.

*Foundation Skills: Effective workers need
the following skills and qualities for solid job
performance—*

- **basic skills** (reading, writing, math, speaking and listening);
- **thinking skills** (thinking creatively, decision making,
  problem solving and knowing how to learn); and
- **personal qualities** (individual responsibility, self-esteem,
  sociability, self-management and integrity).

*Workplace Competencies: Effective workers need to
productively use—*

- **resources** (e.g., allocate time, money, materials, space and
  staff);
- **interpersonal skills** (e.g., work in teams, teach others, serve customers, lead, negotiate and work well with
  people from culturally diverse backgrounds);

- **information** (e.g., acquire and evaluate data, organize and maintain files, interpret and communicate and use computers to process information);

- **systems** (e.g., understand social, organizational, and technological systems; monitor and correct performance; design or improve systems);

- **technology** (e.g., select equipment and tools, apply technology to specific tasks, maintain and troubleshoot equipment).

Teaching students problem-solving skills is important for several reasons, including:

- It **gives students practice at solving problems** that resemble those found in the workplace.

- It **helps students learn a process** that can be applied to many different problems.

- **Problem-solving activities can support all of the SCANS skills.**

- When done with others (in pairs or teams of three to five students), **problem-solving activities help students develop and practice other SCANS skills** (e.g., teamwork, effective communication [being clear, listening, negotiating], responsibility, self-esteem).

By now, you may be saying to yourself, "I already have too much to cover. Now you're telling me to teach more?" The good news is that teaching problem-solving skills doesn't have to be a topic that is singled out and taught in isolation. Instead, it is an instructional strategy that can be used to teach in any subject area. It is recommended that you teach the basics of problem solving first, and then give students opportunities to solve problems related to your course content.

Experienced instructors recommend these steps:

1. **Begin to teach students the basics of problem solving by helping them realize that there is a *process* that**

they already use when encountering everyday problems. Such problems might include fixing a paper jam in a photocopy machine, selecting a long-distance carrier or repairing equipment. So ask them about their everyday problems. Ask questions that require students to describe in detail the steps they take when solving those problems.

2. **Help students isolate the steps involved in the problem-solving process.** If you wish, share the steps described in the IDEAL problem-solving model. It was designed as an aid for teaching and improving problem-solving skills. The IDEAL process includes the following steps:

I = **Identify the problem** (i.e., determine what needs to be done).

D = **Define the problem** (i.e., sharpen and clarify the boundaries).

E = **Explore alternative approaches** (i.e., gather information to determine the available options, analyze and evaluate alternatives, and choose the best one, taking into account many variables, including cost, time, human resources, materials, environment, and expertise).

A = **Act on a plan** (i.e., determine the logical steps to be used and how to progress through the steps).

L = **Look at the result** (i.e., determine whether or not the plan worked).

3. **Develop or choose learning activities that give students opportunities to develop and/or refine their problem-solving skills.** These activities can be related to or separate from the subject area. The options for developing activities that promote problem solving are nearly endless!

The following guidelines may be helpful:

- **Allow students to be at the center of their own learning**. After all, people don't learn how to solve problems by being told the correct solution—they learn by doing.

- **Assign open-ended tasks** (instead of those with one right answer). For example, an assignment to select an effective marketing campaign to meet a given set of criteria is open-ended. So is an assignment to design and build a product that addresses a need.

- **Minimize instructions** so that students are encouraged to invent innovative ways to accomplish their tasks.

- **Provide students with a variety of materials** from which to choose (when appropriate).

- When students have questions, the best response is to **repeat the beginning instructions, without giving further information**. This strategy encourages students to work with teammates to figure out how to reach their goal.

- **Allow plenty of time for students to explore**. As long as students are actively engaged, learning is taking place.

- **Encourage students to share ideas with each other**. This strategy reflects how people solve problems in the workplace—with input from others. Most problem-solving activities lend themselves to having students work individually or in pairs. Occasionally, it is appropriate for students to work in teams of three to five. When students work individually, they should be encouraged to seek others' input.

# An activity to teach the basics of the problem-solving process:

## Design and Build the Highest Tower

Challenge students to build the highest tower they can by using nontraditional materials. For each pair of students, provide two pieces of 8.5" x 11" paper, 10 paper clips, and a pair of scissors. To measure and compare the height of towers, you can use a yardstick or measuring tape.

1.  **Instructions for Students:** Give students the following instructions (and no other information):

    Only the materials provided may be used to build the tower.

    The towers must be free standing; they may not lean against a wall or be held up.

    Towers must be brought to the tape on the wall for measuring (optional).

2.  **Measurement:** Measure the height of each structure as it is finished. When all towers have been measured, announce the winners.

3.  **Discussion:** Have students examine all of the towers. Encourage them to discuss the strategies that made some towers more successful than others. Ask students to describe the problem-solving process they used in designing and building their towers. Write a summary of the process for the whole class to see and agree on.

4.  **Continuation:** Allow time for experimentation by instructing each team to build a second tower. This time, give them 15 minutes to experiment with scratch paper before they actually begin their second construction.

**Related Activities:** Have students do one or more of the following activities:

- Have students follow the parameters of a project budget. Develop a cost reporting sheet and assign monetary values to each material. For example:

- Give each team a budget of $1500. Tell them that the winning team will have the highest tower **and** come in under-budget. In case of a tie, the lowest-cost tower will win.

- Assign values to the materials: paper, $500; paper clip, $100; labor, $10/hour; technical assistance from the instructor, $100/minute.

- Write and present a sales presentation about the tower.

- Describe in writing the problem-solving process used throughout the design project. Include diagrams of the steps taken (if appropriate).

**Variation:** If students need more practice at using the problem-solving process, have student pairs use only newspaper, and no other materials or equipment, to construct the longest possible freestanding bridge.

**Sheri Bidwell** *was a consultant with Connections for Learning, Columbus, OH. With an MA in communication and BS in education from The Ohio State University, she became a reading teacher, trainer and educational consultant who wrote books to help teachers be the best they could be. She passed away in 2011.*

# TOPIC XIV:

## Tips for Teaching Large Classes

By P.D. Lesko

It is almost inevitable that teaching undergraduate courses, particularly introductory courses, means teaching large classes. There is a significant difference between the way in which a large class of 300 is taught as compared to a class of 30 or 50 students.

Teaching a large class is not just a matter of teaching more students at the same time, for the larger class is taught in a larger room with fixed seating, and the extra students make even simple things, such as handing back test papers and assignments, more time-consuming. In addition in large classes students feel anonymous, and are less likely to contribute to classroom discussions.

In their study of large classes Wulff et al. (1987) noted that students commented on the impersonal nature of such classes which led to decreased motivation. A third factor, according to Wulff et al. (1987) was an increase in noise and distractions ("Rude people who come late, leave early, or sit and talk to their buddies."). Cooper and Robinson (2014) write, "It is a sad commentary on our universities that the least engaging class sizes and the least involving pedagogy is foisted upon the students at the most pivotal time of their undergraduate careers: when they are beginning college."

Large class size, then, brings at least three sets of problems with which to deal, namely a more challenging teaching environment, more time-consuming administrative tasks, and a large anonymous, less involved audience. This chapter will give you some ideas as to how to tackle these challenges, and some practical examples of how to teach large undergraduate classes.

### The MOOC Debate: Revolution or Disillusion?

In a 2014 piece published in the *MIT Technology Review*, Justin Pope, a former higher education reporter for the Associated Press, offered an answer to that question. Pope writes:

> A few years ago, the most enthusiastic advocates of MOOCs believed that these "massive open online courses" stood poised to overturn the century-old model of higher education. Their interactive technology promised to deliver top-tier teaching from institutions like Harvard, Stanford, and MIT, not just to a few hundred students in a lecture hall on ivy-draped campuses, but free via the Internet to thousands or even millions around the world. At long last, there appeared to be a solution to the problem of "scaling up" higher education: if it were delivered more efficiently, the relentless cost increases might finally be rolled back. Some wondered whether MOOCs would merely transform the existing system or blow it up entirely. Computer scientist Sebastian Thrun, cofounder of the MOOC provider Udacity, predicted that in 50 years, 10 institutions would be responsible for delivering higher education.
>
> All this activity is beginning to generate interesting data about what MOOCs actually do. In September, MIT physicist David Pritchard and other researchers published a study of *Mechanics Review*, an online course he teaches that is based on an on-campus course of the same name. The authors found that the MOOC was generally effective at communicating difficult material—Newtonian mechanics—even to students who weren't MIT caliber. In fact, the students who started the online course knowing the least about physics showed the same relative improvement on tests as much stronger students. "They may have started with an F and finished with an F," Pritchard says, "but they rose with the whole class."
>
> Education researchers are still just beginning to mine all the data that MOOCs generate about how students respond to the material. Researchers like Pritchard can track every step of every student through a MOOC; he says that for him to study his traditional students that way, "they'd have to carry

a head-cam 24-7." Eventually, such data should yield insights about the best ways to present, sequence, and assess particular subjects. Kevin Carey, who has researched MOOCs as director of education policy at the New America Foundation, points out that today's MOOCs haven't even begun to make serious use of artificial intelligence to personalize courses according to each student's strengths and weaknesses (a surprise considering that pioneers like Thrun and Coursera's Daphne Koller came from AI backgrounds).

For all the hype, MOOCs are really content—the latest iteration of the textbook. And just like a book on a library shelf, they can be useful to a curious passerby thumbing through a few pages—or they can be the centerpiece to a well-taught course. On their own, MOOCs are hardly more likely than textbooks to re-create a quality college education in all its dimensions.

Nearly all MOOCs originate from the world's top universities. Their instructors are accustomed to teaching the brightest students, and may not understand the motivations, academic difficulties and self-discipline of the average student. As for faculty, two-thirds of MOOC professors surveyed by *The Chronicle of Higher Education* in 2013 said they had never taught a fully online course before their first open online class.

While MOOC courses have become an important supplement to classroom learning and a tool for professional development, many educators take the view that, using the metrics by which we judge traditional higher education (prestige, completion rates), MOOCs have not fulfilled their original promise.

## Personalizing Large Classes

In any class, but especially in large classes, it is important to establish an atmosphere which conveys the professor's interest in and accessibility to students and which encourages students to participate.

Many instructors try to "make a large class small" by treating it as such. Methods include walking around the classroom while lecturing, moving toward the student asking a question, helping TAs distribute handouts, and developing other methods that allow you to be closer to the students you are teaching. One instructor holds an "open house" during the first session in which students briefly chat with the TAs and the professor while choosing their lab sections. Group work, described in Topic XI, "Collaborative/Cooperative Learning," can also help create a more intimate atmosphere.

Most of us are reluctant to ask questions or make comments in front of dozens of our peers. When students do ask questions in large classes, it is important that the instructor respond in ways that encourage more questions. Students will not feel comfortable raising questions if they feel scorned, humiliated or embarrassed by a sarcastic response. Responses such as "I'm glad you asked that" or "That's a good question" will encourage students to continue asking questions. If appropriate, you might bring a question raised during office hours or after class into the classroom and mention the student's name, for example, "Ann asked me an interesting question about . . . ". Nonverbal responses such as smiling or nodding can also indicate your support of student questions. When asking students questions, it is important to allow enough time--at least five to ten seconds--for them to consider their response. A number of methods exist that encourage student feedback and questions. A question-answer box set up in the classroom or lab or outside the professor's office allows students to raise questions outside of the classroom. Students can sign their questions or submit them anonymously.

Although it may seem daunting, it is important to attempt to learn your students' names. Methods facilitating this attempt include using a seating chart of students (though this requires that students always sit in the same seat), taking pictures of the students, or having them make name cards that they place in front of them during class. Taking attendance can help you learn their names and shows students that you are interested in doing so. Asking individual students to assist you with demonstrations or other equipment in the class can also help you learn their names. Once you have learned some students' names, use them to show that you are interested in learning the rest.

## Large Class Discussions

Traditionally, lectures do not feature much discussion and in comparison with small classes do less to develop in students' higher-order thinking skills. Discussion asks students to process information they have studied in new ways, for instance, by applying it, evaluating it, or comparing their understanding of it with that of others. Class discussions, either between the instructor and the students or the students themselves, greatly improve students' ability to retain information. Some ways in which discussion has been used successfully in a large class setting are outlined below. Lecture plans should include time for discussion once you have considered what kinds of questions you will ask and the purpose you want the discussion to serve. As mentioned previously, it takes time to figure out what activities work best for you. One suggestion for incorporating discussion into a lecture format is to gradually increase students' participation. The list here is presented in order of increased student involvement.

## Questions

One way to encourage students to engage in thinking about the information being presented is to ask questions. Some instructors use short-answer questions to keep students' attention, such as "And when did the war end? What were other reasons for the Civil War." In asking this kind of question, the instructor waits until some students respond. Another kind of a question is open-ended, such as, "Why did the Civil War end?" When asking a question you do not expect students will be able to answer briefly, it is essential that you pause long enough for them to consider before giving an answer yourself. A third type of question solicits students' opinions, e.g., "What do you think about Locke's assertion of..." or "In your opinion, why..." or "What do you think about ....?"

### Show of Hands, Informal Votes, Short Surveys

Another way to involve students in the presentation of information is to ask for a show of hands or to take an informal vote on a subject or issue. For instance, you might ask, "How many are convinced by Smith's argument?" "How many feel that Golberg's interpretation is reasonble? "This vote may or may not lead to student commentary. A short survey that asks students for their opinions on or familiarity with a topic can be given at the beginning or end of a class. If given at the beginning, the results could be tabulated and analyzed during class. If given at the end, the instructor could tabulate the results and incorporate them into the next lecture.

## Student Discussions and Small Group Work

In these activities, the instructor poses a question or a problem and the students answer by discussing it with one or two fellow students. For instance, after discussing a study, the instructor might ask students if they can think of alternative cases or factors. Students can also be asked to summarize the main points of the lecture. After the allotted time (five or ten minutes), the class reconvenes and volunteers from the groups offer their responses.

## Other Participatory Activities

Discussions can also be facilitated by having a group of students involved in the following activities:

### *Discussion Row*

In a lecture hall, a couple of rows are designated as "discussion rows." The students in these rows are expected to respond to the instructors' questions throughout the lecture. Students might rotate sitting here throughout the semester

### *Discussion Quadran*

The lecture hall might be divided into four quadrants. At different points in the lecture or semester, students from a particular quadrant are asked to respond to questions.

### *Expert Panel*

In this case, a panel of "experts" on a particular topic are asked to respond to the instructor's and students' questions on a topic. Participation on a panel counts as part of the student's grade.

### *Classroom "Talk Show"*

In this activity, several students volunteer to be a guest on the "show." The idea is to represent different points of view by having a varied panel of guests. For instance, in a discussion about slavery, students could take the roles of a slave, a slave owner, an abolitionist, an anti-abolitionist, a priest, etc. Students not role-playing act as the audience and ask questions. The instructor should act as moderator and prepare several questions that will provoke different points of view in case the discussion lulls.

## 5 Tips For Making Large Class Lecturers More Participatory

Asking for student participation highlights the distinction between faculty covering material and students learning it. Student participation often results in covering less material during a semester. Yet it also can mean that students learn more material than in a traditional lecture course, because they truly grasp the fundamentals and have more chances to clear up confusion. Large numbers of students in class does not preclude interaction. The following list of ways to open up lectures to student participation have been used in classes of up to 1200 students, as well as in smaller groups.

1. Begin the course or the lecture by posing a problem and eliciting several answers or solutions from the students. The lecture can then go on to explore and build on the suggestions that emerge from the discussion. For example: "When you think about the definition of epidemiology, what possible applications of this methodology come to mind?" "What are some underlying biological factors for poor health status?" "What are some reasons people may not have health insurance?"

Note: If you decide to invite student participation in lectures, consider beginning with the very first lecture, when norms and expectations for class are being established. It is more difficult to engage students in a large lecture class later if they are accustomed to being silent. If you decide to ask students to participate in lectures later in the term, give a short introduction or explanation about your change in strategy.

2. Create an atmosphere that encourages student participation by using a conversational tone and not criticizing student questions or comments in front of the class. Students take a risk when they

talk; you need to deal tactfully with their contributions. Your body language -- whether you hold yourself in a stiff or relaxed manner -- also influences student participation. Consider moving closer to the students rather than speaking from behind the podium. Explain your reasons for varying the traditional lecture style. Students more willingly participate in class if they understand the rationale behind an approach that may be unfamiliar.

3. Ask questions throughout the lecture, so that the lecture becomes more of a conversation. Asking students to raise their hands (for example, "What is the direction of the data: increasing? decreasing?") is easier than asking them to speak. Questions with surprising answers can engage students' interest (for example, "What is the probability that two people in this room have the same birthday?") Generally, questions are more evocative if you are not looking for one right answer. The most fruitful questions are thought-provoking and, often, counterintuitive. For example, when comparing health indicators of different countries, ask students to guess where the U.S. or their country of origin ranks. Discuss the link between socioeconomic status and health; ask students to predict changes over time. For example, "Do you think it has gotten better or worse in your country over the last twenty years?"

4. For debates in a large group, divide the room into two or four groups, assigning one role or position to each group. Have the groups caucus separately to develop their positions before the debate begins. For example, in discussing the positive and negative aspects of a policy approach or community health intervention, divide the room in half for split brainstorming sessions; one group focusing on the positive and the other focusing on the negative. If there is time, have the groups switch positions. Or use the format of public hearings, with one group representing those who have called the hearings, and other groups representing the different protagonists.

5. Assign a one-minute paper at the end of class. In this exercise, students write down what they consider (a) the main point of the class and (b) the main question they still have as they leave. You can use some of these questions to begin the next lecture, or students can be asked to bring them to section or lab. One advantage of this technique is that students may listen more carefully and review their notes thoughtfully.

**P.D. Lesko** *holds both undergraduate and graduate degrees from the University of Michigan at Ann Arbor. She has taught at the University of Michigan-Dearborn, Wayne State University and Eastern Michigan University.*

# TOPIC XV:

## Diversity in the Classroom

By Andrea Peck

According to the 2014 "American Freshman National Norms," a survey conducted by the UCLA Higher Education Research Institute, "stories focused on faculty's engagement with diversity in the classroom," found that "most (55%) respondents believe that faculty at their institutions are unprepared to address diversity issues in the classroom."

The following comes from "The American Freshman: Forty Year Trends," published by UCLA's Higher Education Research Institute:

> Many changes have occurred in American higher education in the last 40 years. Most significant has been the unprecedented growth in enrollments accompanied by changes in the proportions who are female, who are students of color, who attend full time, and who attend four-year institutions (NCES, 2006). The opening of pathways to the baccalaureate for women, racial/minority students, first-generation college students, and low-income students who had limited opportunity before the 1960s occurred as a result of the civil rights and women's movements and a series of policy initiatives to increase access to higher education.

> The baccalaureate degree has become a minimum and essential credential for employers in a wide array of occupations, as higher education and training beyond high school is no longer optional for those who aspire towards upward social and economic mobility in American life. As a result, we could not have predicted the number of high school graduates who would take advantage of expanded opportunity to higher education. Moreover, higher education enrollments

are projected to continue increasing from 2006 through 2015:

Full-time undergraduate enrollment is expected to continue growing more rapidly than part-time enrollment, and the growth in enrollment at four-year institutions is expected to be greater than at two-year institutions during this period (NCES, 2006).

From 1972 to 2004, college participation rates increased, with high school graduates enrolled in college immediately after high school increasing from 49 to 67 percent (NCES, 2006). Additionally, for the past 35 years, undergraduate enrollment has been larger in four-year institutions than in two-year institutions, and aside from a slowdown in the early 1990s, enrollment has grown fairly steadily at four-year institutions since 1970 (NCES, 2006). These changes were greatly facilitated by the introduction of policy initiatives (e.g., Higher Education Act of 1965 and subsequent reauthorizations; Middle-Income Student Assistance Act of 1978) and financial aid grant and loan programs (e.g., Pell Grants, Perkins Loans, Stafford Loans) that provided aid directly to students to allow them mobility and choice regardless of income.

At the same time that access has reached unprecedented levels, additional issues have emerged that raise serious questions about whether four-year colleges and universities are doing their fair share of achieving educational equity, meeting students' needs and developing students' values, skills, and knowledge that equip them for an increasingly complex and global society. Institutions do not operate entirely autonomously from larger social and political pressures in society. Some contend our higher education system has become more stratified in terms of students and institutions (Bastedo & Gumport, 2003; Astin & Oseguera, 2004), preserving education of the elite in an era of increased access. Our system is strongly driven by economic and market forces that increase competition for resources and talented students, promote the view of students as self-interested consumers who know how to best meet their educational needs, result in declining funds for public higher education, and increase privatization of many previously public services.

At most institutions of higher learning, the student population is diverse. Whether it's a result of age, ethnic, life, work, or learning style differences, it's valuable to recognize these differences and their impact on your classroom.

Carefully consider student demographics when determining course content and the presentation of that content. For instance, in 1967, 80.5 percent of entering first-year students were 18 years old, while only 13.7 percent were 19 and older. By 2023, 19.7 percent of entering students are expected to be 18-19, and 80.3 percent 20 and older, according to projections by the National Center for Education Statistics. From 1976 to 2012, the percentage of Hispanic students rose from 4 percent to 15 percent, the percentage of Asian/Pacific Islander students rose from 2 percent to 6 percent, the percentage of Black students rose from 10 percent to 15 percent, and the percentage of American Indian/Alaska Native students rose from 0.7 to 0.9 percent. During the same period, the percentage of white students fell from 84 percent to 60 percent.

## Universal Design for Learning (UDL)

What follows is an overview in Universal Design for Learning from the Center for Teaching Excellence at Cornell University:

Universal Design for Learning (UDL) is a teaching approach that works to accommodate the needs and abilities of all learners and eliminate unnecessary hurdles in the learning process. This means developing a flexible learning environment in which information is presented in multiple ways, students engage in learning in a variety of ways, and students are provided options when demonstrating their learning.

Universal design for learning is similar to "universal instructional design" or UID, and 'universal design for instruction' or UDI. All three advocate for accessible and inclusive instructional approaches that meet the needs and abilities of all learners.

There are three main principles of UDL:

1. **Provide Options for Perception**—Based on the premise that learners access information differently, this principle means providing flexible and multiple ways to present information. For example, using PowerPoint as a visual supplement to your lecture.

2. **Provide Options for Expression**—Since learners vary in their abilities to demonstrate their learning in different ways, this principle means providing flexible and multiple ways to allow students to express their knowledge or demonstrate their skills. For example, providing students an option of writing a final exam or submitting a final assignment.

3. **Provide Options for Comprehension**—Students are motivated to learn for different reasons and vary in the types of learning activities that keep them engaged. This third principle means providing multiple ways for engaging in course activities. For example, engaging students in both group work activities and individual work, as opposed to engaging students only in individual work.

Giving choices, however, does not mean changing expectations. For example, if your course learning outcomes include being able to communicate in writing, it is not possible to offer students the option of demonstrating their learning through an oral presentation rather than through a written assignment.

Students differ in the ways that they perceive and comprehend information that is presented to them. This principle tells us that by showing the same material in different ways, learning opportunities are increased for all. What is important to keep in mind is: if these "multiple" options are not there, there is an increased chance to inhibit student learning.

## Engaging Diversity in the Classroom

The following tips are taken from Barbara Gross Davis's chapter entitled "Diversity and Complexity in the Classroom: Considerations of Race, Ethnicity and Gender" in her excellent book, *Tools for Teaching*.

Davis writes: "There are no universal solutions or specific rules for responding to ethnic, gender, and cultural diversity in the classroom…. Perhaps the overriding principle is to be thoughtful and sensitive…." She recommends that you, the teacher:

- Recognize any biases or stereotypes you may have absorbed.

- Treat each student as an individual, and respect each student for who he or she is.

- Rectify any language patterns or case examples that exclude or demean any groups.

- Do your best to be sensitive to terminology that refers to specific ethnic and cultural groups as it changes.

- Get a sense of how students feel about the cultural climate in your classroom. Tell them that you want to hear from them if any aspect of the course is making them uncomfortable.

- Introduce discussions of diversity at department meetings.

- Become more informed about the history and culture of groups other than your own.

- Convey the same level of respect and confidence in the abilities of all your students.

- Don't try to "protect" any group of students. Don't refrain from criticizing the performance of individual students in your class on account of their ethnicity or gender. And be evenhanded in how you acknowledge students' good work.

- Whenever possible, select texts and readings whose language is gender-neutral and free of stereotypes, or cite the shortcomings of material that does not meet these criteria.

- Aim for an inclusive curriculum that reflects the perspectives and experiences of a pluralistic society.

- Do not assume that all students will recognize cultural, literary or historical references familiar to you.

- Bring in guest lecturers to foster diversity in your class.

- Give assignments and exams that recognize students' diverse backgrounds and special interests.

## Returning Students

When presenting topics for a classroom discussion, use time frames, experiences and names with which a variety of students would be familiar. While returning (older) students may relate to information that enables them to reminisce about the past, as well as enjoy learning about the present, younger students may prefer topics that directly impact them now. References should be as inclusive as possible with respect to student demographics.

In understanding students' attitudes and behaviors, keep in mind that many returning students were educated in structured classroom settings. As a result, they're accustomed to formal lecture and discussion formats. Their younger counterparts, the Facebook generation, have had more external stimulation and will expect an active, entertaining learning approach. Thus, incorporate a variety of activities and visual aids to liven up your classroom and to appeal to a plethora of student interests and tastes.

Returning students bring a variety of qualities—extensive life and work experiences and a clear focus and determination—to the classroom. Because most are attending college for the first time or returning to upgrade job positions and skills, they value their education. As a result, they're more likely than younger students to participate in the class. Capitalize on their desire to be vocal and to take initiative. Provide a forum for their feedback and interactions. And though younger students may be more familiar with course curricula, they may be less confident about their educational goals. Consequently, you may need to encourage them to be more active classroom participants.

Like age, gender and ethnic differences affect the classroom. White students represented 90.9 percent of the first-time, full-time freshmen in 1971 and their proportion declined to 60.3 percent in 2012, indicating proportional increases in the representation of other racial/ethnic groups and demographic shifts in the U.S. population. Most notably, Asian American/Asian students' representation has nearly doubled each decade, constituting 0.6 percent of freshmen in 1971 and by 2012 representing 6.3 percent of all college students.

Similarly, although they are more likely than other groups to begin at community colleges, the percentage of Latinos entering baccalaureate-granting institutions has also steadily increased, due primarily to sheer demographic growth. Their representation among first-time, full-time freshmen increased from .06 percent in 1971 to 15 percent in 2012, with trends indicating their representation doubled from 1971 to 1980 and then tripled from 1990 to 2000.

The percentage of incoming students reporting a learning disability was 11 percent in 2011 (the most recent year the National Center for Education Statistics asked about disabilities) – more than 20 times the 0.5 percent reported in 1983. This increase in the proportion of learning-disabled students entering college is mirrored in similar trends in elementary and secondary school populations (NCES, 2011).

Approach your students' learning with respect by refraining from generalizing, criticizing or praising anyone in particular and by treating all students fairly. Most of all, be sensitive.

In addition to social, personal, and genetic differences, students have different learning styles. Extroverted learners learn best by interacting. These students like to express and exchange ideas because it enables them to sort through and understand them better. They'll benefit from open discussions and opportunities to interact with you and others right away.

Introverted learners need time to process ideas and concepts. They learn best by writing information down and then reviewing it later before they address you with any questions. These students work well independently, even within a group, on projects, or on class assignments.

The literal learner responds best to hands-on learning experiences that enable him or her to know something by actually doing it. Math, science and technology can be good subject areas for these students. They benefit from role playing and experiential learning as well.

Abstract learners respond best to creative assignments that allow them to discover and explore new and different perspectives on their topic. They like to learn and theorize about ideas through analogy, comparison, and metaphor. Writing, group discussions, and debates as well as a variety of artistic endeavors support their learning styles.

Some students are driven by accomplishment and will take on greater amounts of work the more they are expected to do. Extra credit and/or extra work requirements for higher grades motivate them. These students prefer to complete assignments prior to moving onto something new and having ample time to complete their work when or before it's due.

Finally, there are those students who like to work on a myriad of projects simultaneously. They have a tendency to get scattered, so keep them on task to ensure work completion. Their optimal performance will come as a result of having several assignments due as opposed to one or two major projects. They perform well under last minute time pressures.

Today, the classroom is comprised of heterogeneous audiences who not only learn in different ways, but who respond to and benefit from a variety of teaching approaches. As a result, instructors need to approach learning as diversely as the students who sit before them.

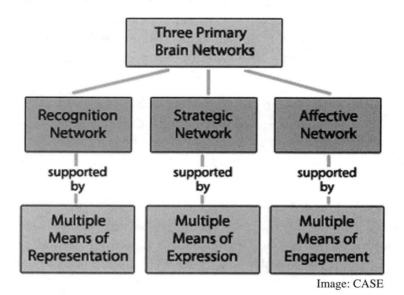

Image: CASE

Teaching courses using any distance education technology requires that new skills be learned or that existing skills be sharpened. Faculty will need to develop additional instructional strategies for achieving learning objectives. Irrespective of the delivery medium, maintaining consistent multiple forms of interaction is important to ensure the success of distance education students. Creating opportunities for various forms of text-based interaction using computer-mediated tools whether student-to-student, student-to-group, student-to-class, or student-to-instructor is important to replicate the traditional classroom experience. Each of these forms of interaction, both textual and videoconferenced, can be facilitated using distance education technology.

Proven competencies for effective teaching at a distance are course planning and organization, verbal and nonverbal presentation skills, collaborative teamwork, questioning strategies, subject-matter expertise and coordination of student activities at field sites (Soluski & Vai, 2015). Course planning and organization involve understanding the different advantages and disadvantages of the delivery medium and its effect on the course design.

The widespread use of distance education technology presents new challenges and opportunities for adjunct faculty. Higher education has embraced each new distance education technology medium which has resulted from advancements in the telecommunications industry, from the telecourse to Moodle. To be competitive and be in a position to advance the educational institution's strategic goals, adjunct faculty will need to also embrace these technologies.

*Contributed by:* **Tinnie A. Banks** *of Lorain County Community College, Elyria, OH.*

# TOPIC XVI:

## Preparing to Teach Online and Hybrid Courses

By Tinnie A. Banks

So, your teaching schedule calls for you to teach an online course. It doesn't matter if this is your first such venture, or you have taught at a distance before—it should be approached as if it were your first ever. Recall that when you decided to enter the teaching profession, you looked to the human interaction with students as a major factor in your decision. You were to be the conductor, and every class a symphony with lots of direction and emotion involved in the production (class). Now you are about to enter a different arena. As such, you must view yourself as an engineer on a train. The train has many cars—each is loaded with different course delivery technologies which you will need to call upon to reach your destination (objectives). The goods you must deliver, the students, are in the last car. Sometimes, you can't even see them.

This topic will provide you the information necessary to complete your journey—through the use of technology. However, as with teaching face-to-face, preparation is necessary. In fact, perhaps it's even slightly more important. In a classroom, it is easy to recover from a mishap or an error; in a distance learning situation, it is much more difficult. There are two major factors that you must keep in mind while preparing for your distance education courses: you must have complete command of the technology, and you must not lose sight of the fact that the human touch alluded to earlier is not de-emphasized, but is, in fact, emphasized as much as possible.

Master the technology, but do not get so wrapped up in it that individual students are neglected! The same basic premises apply to a distance education course—keep the lines of communication open, and always be well prepared.

Preparing to teach online courses has additional administrative and pedagogical considerations. Administrative policies concerning intellectual property rights and course ownership are an integral component of teaching at a distance, especially when preparation is expected to include development of course content. Unlike a traditional course, teaching a distance education course will necessitate interaction with additional instructional technology support personnel who may work outside of the academic department.

Distance education technology can be either synchronous or asynchronous. Synchronous distance education technologies include live streaming coupled with chat, web conference tools such as Blackboard, Adobe Connect, Skype, etc..... A synchronous course meets at a designated time in multiple locations that are closer to the student than commuting to the main campus. Face-to-face interaction between students and instructor remains an integral component of synchronous courses. When comparing distance education technologies, those taught using synchronous technologies are most similar to the traditional on-campus course. Although some existing instructional materials from the traditional course can be reused, preparation time needs to include strategies to maintain interaction and the attention of the students located at the remote sites.

Asynchronous distance education technologies are characterized by anytime, anyplace learning, provide flexibility and convenience for both students and instructors. With an asynchronous course, there is no designated class meeting time or classroom, but students can access instructional materials anytime and anyplace. Asynchronous learning tools include email, electronic mailing lists, threaded conferencing systems, online discussion boards, wikis, and blogs.

## Course Management Systems (CMS)

A course management system (CMS) is a collection of software tools providing an online environment for course interactions. A CMS includes a variety of online tools and environments, such as:

- An area for faculty posting of class materials such as course syllabus and handouts;

- An area for student posting of papers and other assignments;

- A gradebook where faculty can record grades and each student can view his or her grades;

- An integrated email tool allowing participants to send announcement email messages to the entire class or to a subset of the entire class;

- A chat tool allowing synchronous communication among class participants;

- A threaded discussion board allowing asynchronous communication among participants.

In addition, a CMS is typically integrated with other databases in the university so that students enrolled in a particular course are automatically registered in the CMS as participants in that course.

Institutions will differ in their investment in distance education technologies, directly impacting opportunities for securing a distance education assignment. Prior to accepting the assignment, thoroughly understand the institution's intellectual property and ownership policy for course development. Institutions vary on compensation for development of distance education courses and ownership rights. Some institutions rely on "work for hire" policies. This means that work done by a faculty member under contract belongs to the institution.

Other institutions have policies that include joint ownership and revenue sharing, similar to patent agreements. At other times, the faculty can negotiate to retain all copyrights—even of instructional materials (Boettcher, 1999). Cash or hiring faculty on an overload basis are all possibilities for course development.

Irrespective of the delivery method, teaching with distance education technology requires advanced planning and preparation. Depending on the delivery medium, it may also require additional training and development of course materials such an audio or video lectures. There are pedagogical issues to consider when designing new instructional materials for a distance education course. Distance learning requires three things not always found in traditional classroom teaching: a) learner-centered design, b) learner-centered delivery skills, and c) direct learner participation (Smaldino & Simonson, 2014). New instructional strategies will need to be integrated into the design of course materials which focus on student-centered learning.

Seek and take advantage of training opportunities, both in and outside of the educational institution, to learn more about distance education technologies. Training may include seminars and workshops focusing on a particular distance delivery medium or on strategies for course development. Learn about any software and hardware standards in place for course design and development. In addition to the technical skills required to operate the equipment or software specific to the medium, competencies for distance teaching include course planning and organization, verbal and nonverbal presentation skills, collaborative teamwork, questioning strategies, subject matter expertise, student involvement and coordination of their activities at field sites (Soluski & Vai, 2015).

Develop course materials with interactivity in mind. How this is accomplished directly depends on the delivery medium. Vella (2007) identifies three types of interactions:

- interactions that occur between the learner and the instructor,
- interactions that occur among learners, and
- interactions that take place between learners and the content they are trying to master.

Interactions enable active learner participation in the instructional/ training/performance improvement process. They allow learners to tailor learning experiences to meet their specific needs or abilities. Interactions enable clarification and transfer of new ideas to already held concept frameworks. Interactions promote intrinsic motivation on the part of a learner by highlighting the relevance that new information may have under these circumstances (Wagner, 1997). When designing instructional strategies for distant students, the following types of interactions should be considered, interactions:

- to increase participation,

- to develop communication,

- to receive feedback,

- to enhance elaboration and retention,

- to support learner control/self-regulation,

- to increase motivation,

- for negotiation and clarification of understanding,

- for team building, and

- for discovery and exploration.

Request information about course evaluation processes for the students, course and instructor. Gain an understanding of long standing policies concerning proctored examinations requirements or online testing procedures. For course evaluations, the academic department may use the same criteria and forms used in the traditional course, along with an addendum to accommodate the use of technology and delivery medium. Conversely, there may be a completely distinct evaluation process. Track ongoing, informal feedback from students for future or immediate revisions of course materials. The first time a course is delivered, there are bound to be some glitches. Be sure to test developed course materials from the student's perspective prior to allowing student access. Problems requiring few resources, which can be resolved quickly, should take priority. Proactively keep the students informed about any problems or changes to previously communicated syllabus and weekly schedule information.

The ever increasing availability of distance education programs and courses has simultaneously increased opportunities for teaching assignments. These assignments may include a mixture of traditional and distance education courses. While there are some similarities between these delivery mediums, the primary difference is that distance education courses require more advance preparation and up-front information gathering to gain an understanding of the institution's administrative policies governing their distance education courses. Although instruction using distance education technologies may initially require more time, ultimately the instructor will benefit as expectations and roles are clarified, resulting in an effective and efficient course design, development and delivery.

Once you've been hired to teach an online course in your field, and have received the syllabus and textbooks, there is more you need to know. Listed below are some questions you may want to ask the Department Chair or Program Director before you begin compiling materials for your online course.

## Faculty Checklist

1. What kind of faculty training is offered? Is this training required? Is an electronic competency test required for faculty and/or for students?

2. Which course management software is used?

3. What kinds of automation are available for the instructor?

4. What are the software and hardware requirements for faculty? What are the software and hardware requirements for students?

5. Will I be reimbursed for Internet service?

6. What kind of technical support and help are available for adjunct faculty and for students? How soon can I expect a response when I have a problem?

7. What passwords are needed for course and electronic library access?

8. How much of the course content is proscribed?

9. What are my job responsibilities (online training, course design or updating, office hours, live chat, online departmental meetings, minimum number of days online each week)?

10. How quickly am I expected to respond to student emails and postings?

11. What are the limits on class size?

12. Are faculty and students required to post online a certain number of days per week?

13. Is student attendance monitored electronically?

14. Which electronic textbooks available?

15. How do I get the course texts (request from contact person, bookstore, publisher)?

16. Is exam proctoring required?

17. How are grades submitted?

18. Who is my contact person? How does this person prefer to be contacted (phone, email, online troubleshooting form)?

19. Who are some of the other part-time (and full-time) instructors teaching this course online? Are they willing to assist new adjuncts?

20. Who owns my course?

21. Am I eligible to apply for course development stipends? What is the application procedure?

**Tinnie A. Banks** *is a retired Instructional Design Media Coordinator who worked for many years at Lorain County Community College, Elyria, OH.*

*In Their Own Words*

"In Their Own Words" essays are written by administrators, tenured and non-tenured faculty members who work at a variety of two- and four-year colleges and universities. We are grateful to these educators for sharing their insights and their expertise.

## Testing Process

One of the most time-consuming, tedious tasks for a beginning instructor is the preparation, administration, and scoring of tests. He or she may wonder if there is not an easier way to handle the testing process. Have veteran instructors discovered " tricks of the trade" which would make the testing process easier? This article will answer some of the questions regarding the preparation, the administration, and the scoring of the test.

The instructor has to make several decisions in planning for testing, such as the following:

- **When and how often should tests be given?**
  The approximate number of tests and tentative times for tests should be decided when the course or unit is planned. There should not be too many or too few tests, based primarily on the nature of the course.

- **What kinds of questions or items should be used?**
  The types of test items selected must be appropriate to the subject matter of the course. The instructor must consider his or her instructional objectives and the nature of the content covered. It would be wise to use a combination of test types. The strengths and weaknesses of each type should be considered in relationship

to the objectives since some formats are less appropriate than others for measuring certain objectives.

### ✌ How long should the test be?

The length of the test will vary depending upon the length of the testing time, the amount of material being covered, and the types of questions being used. Remember, a test should only sample the body of material being tested. Essay questions may be easier to compose than objective-type questions, but they are very time consuming for students to complete and instructors to score. Typically, one essay question may take longer for students to complete than 50 multiple-choice items. In developing objective-type questions, allow one minute for every two true/false items and one minute for each multiple-choice item. There should be sufficient time for all students to complete the test within the allotted time without feeling rushed. Another consideration in the test length is to design it so that the instructor is able to score the tests and return them within the next one or two class meetings, while the test material is still fresh on the students' minds. The more time that goes by, the less the students care about the questions they missed. Also, if the instructor scores the tests immediately, he or she is able to determine whether the students are ready to move onto new material.

### ✌ What emphasis should be given to the various aspects of the content?

Emphasis on various areas of content in a test should be in the same proportion to the emphasis in the instructional program. If a instructor spends 30 minutes explaining a principle which he or she considered to be important, then there should be sufficient coverage of the principle on the test. There should be no "trick" questions. The test should not be so easy or so hard that it does not discriminate between those who know the content and those who don't.

**≈ In what order should the test items be placed?**

The type of question used, the difficulty of the items, and the content should be considered. Each section should be limited to one test type—for example, a section of true/false, then a section of multiple choice, then matching. The arrangement requires fewer directions, and it is easier for the students because they can retain the same mind set throughout each section. Ideally, the test should be arranged from simple to more complex. This arrangement gives the students confidence; otherwise, they may become frustrated if they are given very complex questions at the beginning of the test.

**≈ What about the use of tests developed by the textbook publisher or test bank questions?**

It will certainly save a great deal of preparation time to utilize these sources; however, be sure to use questions from the test bank which are representative of the content that has been taught. It is virtually impossible for any instructor to use a complete publisher-generated test without making at least some modifications. If students realize that tests are always publisher-generated, then the motivation to listen to the instructor will be diminished.

**≈ What about an answer key?**

A key for the test should be prepared when the test is developed. If some items have more than one correct answer, all possible responses should be included. The test questions should be very clear in meaning; they should not be misinterpreted by the students. However, despite one's best efforts, students occasionally misunderstand a question. In this case, the instructor should be willing to allow alternate answers and not penalize the students for their answers.

**≈ What about the test reproduction?**

The test should be reproduced in a very legible form and be free from typographical errors. Don't crowd the items on the page. Ideally, instructors should double space between test items. Allow sufficient space for the students to provide their answers. In addition, write very clear instructions for each part. The directions should indicate what the students are to do, how they are to do it, and where they should record their answers. It is very beneficial to indicate the point value of each question in each section so students can know how to manage their time.

**Must an instructor observe the students during the test?**

Yes, it is imperative that instructors always observe the students as they take the test. There should be no opportunity for students to cheat. Instructors must not leave the room or get so busy at their desk that they are not aware of what is going on. Some instructors prepare scrambled forms of the same tests when students sit close together. As much as possible, make the room conducive to good test taking; for example, adequate light and temperature, quietness, and sufficient work space. Instructors may want to remind students of the remaining time available or write the minutes left on the chalkboard.

**What about using Scantron answer sheets and scoring machines?**

By all means use these sources if they are available. This process speeds up the grading of the objective part of the test considerably. In addition, many scoring machines can generate an item analysis of the questions. If there is no Scantron available, have students write their responses to the objective questions on an answer sheet. This will speed up scoring considerably, and the instructor may be able to use the tests later without further duplication.

**What purpose does an item analysis serve?**

Item analysis allows the instructor to determine the effectiveness of each test item. After the scoring of the test has been completed, the instructor should do an item analysis, unless the scoring machine has already done it. Record the number of time each question was missed. If an item is never missed or was missed by everyone, then it serves no purpose. If many students made a perfect score, the test was probably too easy. On the other hand, if a high percentage of the class made a failing score, it was probably too hard. Some experts recommend that instructors make three stacks with their graded test papers—the top one-third, the middle one-third, and the bottom one-third. Compare those questions missed by each group. Occasionally, there may be a question that the poorer students got right but the better students missed. Go back and study the way the test question was written for a clue as to why this happened.

Although the testing process represents a great deal of time, it allows instructors to evaluate the students and to determine if the students have understood the material. Instructors must become skilled in the test construction process since it is so important in the educational environment.

When instructors return the test, students can give them interesting insight into how they interpreted the question or how the wording was confusing. If the instructor collects the test, not ever allowing tests to circulate, this information can be used to revise the test before giving it again at some future date. However, giving the same test year after year is not wise. The same test just doesn't fit as each time one's teaching and class makeup change but it is not necessary to compose a completely new test each time either.

*Contributed by:* **Mary Alice Griffin** and **Donnie McGahee** of Valdosta State University, Valdosta, GA.

*"I revised it, but don't think for a second
I changed anything <u>you</u> wanted changed."*

# TOPIC XVII:

## Testing Strategies

By M.B. McKinley

Tests let both faculty and students gauge learning mastery and provide a chance for more learning. Tests should be designed with primary course objectives in mind; they should cover what has gone on in sections (usually) and lectures. What follows are some guidelines for the types of information to consider while developing a course and the accompanying tests or quizzes.

Before making up an exam, go over the kinds of information and skills emphasized in the course. Was the memorization of facts or the application of principles more important? The exam should be constructed accordingly. Students should be told in advance, preferably at the beginning of the semester, what kinds of exams will be given in a course. If the course is a long-running one, some students may have access to old exams; thus, it is probably fairer to give all students sample copies of at least one previous exam, or use the samples for review. If the instructor is new to the course, old tests can be a useful resource to see what topics were addressed and how they were covered.

Frequent testing enhances learning and provides information on student progress. For maximum learning from an exam, and out of respect for the students, tests should be returned as soon as possible. Unless we intend to discuss them in class, we should hand tests back at the end of a period in order to avoid students being preoccupied by them.

It is an academic truism that classroom tests may be considered further learning experiences, as well as a differential measure of "learning/knowledge." To enhance the "learning" features which can occur with multiple-choice tests, the following represent three testing/learning-enhanced strategies:

1.  provide students with the opportunity to use a **personal dictionary** while taking the test;

2.  allow **"crib notes"** be used during the test and/or

3.  permit **textbook use** for "open book" tests.

First, encourage students to bring a personal dictionary to the test so that they may look up any words they do not fully comprehend. In surveying students who have used the dictionary during tests, it was found that the words most commonly looked up are those of a general vocabulary kind. In other words, while they may look up technical vocabulary pertinent to course content, most use the dictionary for everyday words, e.g. ambiguity, complimentary, virtually, condone, delete, etc.

The major thrust of the use of a dictionary is that it enhances test validity. It may be reasonably assumed that students come to the test with varying levels of vocabulary sophistication—the use of a dictionary tends to flatten out these differences. Students who miss a particular test item can then be assumed to have erred because of lack of content knowledge and not because of a less sophisticated general vocabulary. After all, test validity means assessing course-related material.

A second strategy which can supplement learning in a multiple-choice testing environment is the use of "crib notes"—self-written notes designed to aid the student in answering test questions. One method of doing crib notes is to offer the student the opportunity to write anything and everything they can on both sides of a 5" x 8" index card and bring that single card to the test. Students who have participated in this testing strategy have reported almost universal endorsement of the idea. The most commonly cited benefit of the crib notes was that preparing the notes by looking for critical concepts, ideas, terms, etc. forced the student to analyze and synthesize information to a far greater degree than "just memorizing the material."

A third assessment approach which can be considered a further learning aid in a testing environment is to give "open-book" tests. Open book tests more closely resemble the real world outside the

hallowed halls of academia. Effective problem solving and associated learning in the working world requires that successful persons
know where and how to use the resources available—the textbook
is a perfect resource for test taking! Some clear advantages that ac-
crue to open-book testing:

1. students **rely less on memorizing facts and rely
   more on learning**, understanding, retaining, and applying concepts and principles;

2. students with abilities other than rote learning will
   have **a more equalized opportunity to succeed**; and

3. test questions can more **readily measure syntheses,
   analyses,** and allow for judgments.

**Note:** Some faculty will protest that with an open book test students
will not come to class. Not true, a student simply does not have
the time to look up "everything" during the test and the instructor
can include in lectures and discussions material that will be on the
test as well.

An instructor may use all three of the testing strategies noted above
or any combination thereof. For example, an instructor may have students use the "crib notes" along with a personal dictionary, thereby
"doubling" the advantages over just one technique. Regardless of
which ideas are used there are some general issues involving these
testing strategies.

Student anxiety is a well-documented inhibitor of optimum test performance. Students have forever complained about the frustration
and lack of control they feel in testing situations. If students feel
such lack of control and the optimum test performance is inhibited,
then the validity of the test is called into question. Students with an
increased sense of well-being (less anxiety/frustration) as provided
by the three assessment strategies, will in all likelihood do better on
the tests, and more importantly, learn during the test. However and
relatedly, faculty will be required to construct or select from test
banks a better grade of questions to realize the maximum benefits
of these alternative testing formats.

There is one great unanswered question remaining and that is:

**Is the opportunity for student dishonesty during
the test (cheating) more likely with any or all of
these testing strategies?**

It has been the author's experience in having used all three testing
formats that there is no known increased likelihood of academic
dishonesty. After all, the dictionary, crib-notes and/or open books
legitimately provide the resources that students might otherwise be
tempted to use dishonestly. Indeed, a strong case can be made that
the use of such techniques have, in actuality, reduced the motivation to "cheat" as the student thinks the testing strategy is more
compassionate, just and fair.

A final note on multiple-choice tests themselves. Whether an instructor creates his or her own test questions from "scratch" or selects
questions from a test bank, there are a number of points to keep
in mind so that the resultant test works in achieving its intended
purpose(s) regardless of the testing strategy employed. Here is a
short list of some of those points:

1. Do questions relate to a learning outcome(s)?

2. Are the questions written in "correct" English, e.g. a/an
   before a vowel?

3. Have the foils (answers) been arranged in a systematic
   fashion, such as alphabetically or length of answer?

4. Are correct answers roughly balanced as to the number
   of A's, B's, C's and D's?

5. Have negative questions been avoided? Or, if used (spar-
   ingly!), has the negative been underlined or bolded?

6. Does the test start with a couple of confidence-building
   questions?

7. Are there some "humorous" items scattered throughout
   the test as anxiety reducers?

8. Are some items personalized, e.g. identifies the instructor
   with the material, class?

9. Have so-called "tricky" items been avoided?

Ideally, multiple-choice questions should be geared to take about 45 seconds per question and the questions themselves should not be comprised of more than four foils each—a fifth foil detracts from test validity!

All in all, the author has been using a combination of the above noted testing strategies over many years and while no single one of the techniques works best in all situations, each has proved its worth in some circumstances. From most quarters then, such strategies may work for some testing environs. Come to think of it, there is little or no reason the three strategies can not be used in an essay test mode, is there?

**M.B. McKinley** *is a retired Instructional Design Media Coordinator who worked for many years at Lorain County Community College, Elyria, OH.*

# TOPIC XVIII:

## Testing and Grading

By Donald Greive

One of the most important aspects of a student's education is the testing and grading practices of the instructor. Too often students are conditioned to the sole purpose of trying to determine the responses wanted on the instructor's tests. In addition to student evaluation, the testing process should also be an evaluation of instruction and improvement in the teaching/learning situation. It is important that the testing process incorporate a strategy of reinforcing student successes and positive experiences as well as identifying weaknesses. Unfortunately, in the past, testing was used for a variety of purposes that often raised the anxieties of the students. This included the elimination of students from more difficult and demanding programs, disciplines and courses as well as to rank students for class standing and scholarship qualifications. These and other factors have a direct effect upon student behaviors, including anxiety, during the testing process.

It is important that you as the instructor make every effort to prepare students at the beginning of the course for your testing plan. This starts by informing students on the first day of the class of the testing procedure that you will use, the times that tests will be given, and the content (determined by class objectives) upon which the students will be tested. This avoids the age-old complaint of students that "he or she didn't test over what they talked about in class."

In summary, the ideal reasons that tests are given should be:

1. to reveal to students their areas of strengths and success,

2. to indicate to the instructor the students' progress,

3. to provide motivation for students,

this question: Did students who received high percentage scores on the total test also respond in a similar percentage of correct answers on the questions analyzed? Obviously, if the A students received 90 percent correct answers and above and only 50 percent correct responses on the questions being analyzed it could be assumed it probably is not a valid question.

Item analysis is a simple technique quickly conducted and probably underutilized. It is a very simple process to determine the validity of questionable test items and provides you the opportunity to re-word or rephrase the question so that it more accurately reflects the intent. As was indicated earlier, the simple process described here is not intended to be statistically foolproof, however, it is certainly an improvement over the possibility of guessing when considering such validity, or worse, the possibility of leaving an invalid question or series of questions in an otherwise effective instrument.

## Test Validity

The validity of a test is determined by answering the very simple question, "Am I testing what I should be testing?" Probably in many of the classes that you attended as an undergraduate, the validity of the tests were in question. Too often course preparations were not structured in a way that testing was consistent with the discussions that took place in the class or in the course objectives. This very often happens in classes where instructors use tests over and over. In modern class planning, which requires that each course has objectives, validity becomes less of a problem. To maintain validity in a testing situation, you must be certain that your evaluation instrument and questions on it are based upon the objectives written for the course.

## Test Comprehensiveness

Obviously, the comprehensiveness of a test is important in evaluating students. A test that is not comprehensive will be neither valid nor objective. To test students on a small sample of what has been taught during the course is unfair to students who may not completely grasp that segment of the course, but have mastery over the class in general. *Again, comprehensiveness is not a problem if objectives are written to cover a broad spectrum of the major purposes of the course and the test is developed from those objectives.* You must be careful to make certain that the test adequately samples all the content which has been taught. The development of a broad body of questions, covering the entire course and then selecting from those questions at evaluation time, can assure comprehensiveness without repetition of questions.

## Essay Exams

Essay tests are still one of the most popular colleges tests. They are effective at any level of the learning hierarchy. That is, analysis and synthesis are usually incorporated into the essay questions. Although essay tests require considerable time for students to respond, they do give an in-depth perspective of overall student ability. The essay test is an excellent opportunity for you to interact directly and personally with students. Essay tests can be returned with comments and suggestions and can incorporate creativity, problem solving, and critical thinking skills. Essay tests give significant insight into what the students are learning and what they are hearing in the classroom.

There are several factors to remember when writing test questions that require essay answers. First and foremost is that essay questions should be related to the written course objectives. They should, if possible, be related to the objectives at the analysis or synthesis level. Secondly, essay questions should incorporate a significant amount of content. Realizing that the students will take a long time to respond, questions should be worded so that excessive time is not spent on trivial matters. Finally, you must be certain that in terms of vocabulary, content, and subject covered, the student has sufficient background to respond adequately to the question being asked and that the question is not ambiguous or deceptive.

Essay questions, if constructed and graded properly, are the most accurate of the possible testing techniques. In recent years, despite most teachers resorting to some type of objective grading system, the essay question still leaves considerable latitude for students of ability to express themselves beyond the minimum required competencies. Although this also runs the risk of allowing professional jargon, it usually allows some degree of objectiveness and can be used in a positive manner if controlled by the objectives of the course. Individuals who develop a high degree of skill in writing essay questions find that they can allow for a degree of flexibility.

Grading essay questions presents the greatest problem. You must keep in mind that essay questions are asking students to be objective, yet to generalize. The appropriate way to judge an essay response is to write the response from a faculty viewpoint, listing important comments in priority. Assigning points to the prioritized criteria will then lead to a degree of grading objectivity. You must be cautious, however, that essay questions do not ask for student opinions. Theoretically, if one is merely asking for an opinion, every student should get a perfect score.

### Advantages of Essay Questions

There are numerous advantages as well as disadvantages in testing using essay questions. The most obvious advantages are:

1. They provide in-depth coverage of material or content presented in the class.
2. They allow students maximum utilization of their capabilities in responding to an issue.
3. They are quick and simple to prepare.
4. They can be changed from class to class without greatly affecting the purpose of the question.

### Disadvantages of Essay Questions

The disadvantages of testing using essay questions are:

1. They restrict measurable subject matter.
2. They are time consuming for students.
3. They have a tendency to weigh too heavily a specific part of the course at the expense of other parts.
4. They present the burden of handwriting, spelling, vocabulary, and grammar upon the student.
5. They have a tendency toward subjectivity in evaluation.
6. They are difficult to grade.

## Multiple-Choice Tests

With the advent of computerized scoring and large classes, multiple-choice tests probably are the most predominately used tests in college classrooms today. Not only has the influx of large class instruction and differing class sizes nearly mandated the use of a quickly graded objective system, the capability of providing statistical analysis concerning individual questions is easily obtained from a computerized multiple-choice test. In fact, computer programs exist which allow the instructor to change multiple-choice tests for different classes of the same course. This is accomplished by developing a large database of questions and randomly selecting from the database.

Multiple-choice tests are valuable in that they can measure discrimination abilities between answers as well as simple knowledge. Students with poor handwriting or verbal abilities are not burdened by these unrelated factors which might alter their grades otherwise.

The development of multiple-choice questions is not a simple matter. First, the multiple-choice question should deal with a significant aspect of the course and not be general in nature. You must be careful not to include what may be interpreted as "trick" or misleading questions. It is also important that words not be used in the question that are not understood by all students in the course. Also, present the multiple-choice question in a positive rather than a negative manner.

The actual construction of the multiple-choice tests has several general guidelines. They include:

- do not include answers that are obviously correct or incorrect,
- be sure the correct answers are scattered throughout the response mechanism,
- have no more than four alternative answers with the possibility being right,
- do not use "all of the above" or "none of the above," and
- do not use the terms never, always, likely, or similar adjectives that may divert the meaning for the student.

## Advantages of Multiple-Choice Tests

In deciding the type of question to use for your evaluation tests, you must consider the advantages and disadvantages. The advantages of multiple-choice questions are:

1. They **can cover a broad scope of work** in a short time.

2. They measure the **abilities of students to recognize appropriate responses** rather than recall facts. (This is a significant benefit to older students who sometimes may have difficulty recalling things that they have learned).

3. They are **more valid than some other kinds of tests** and can be easily statistically checked for validity.

4. Students can be **tested at the analysis and synthesis level.**

5. They are **easy to grade.**

6. They **are easily made comprehensive** in nature.

## Disadvantages of Multiple-Choice Tests

The disadvantages of multiple-choice questions are:

1. There is a **tendency to construct most responses** toward the learned knowledge.

2. The **questions are time consuming and difficult to develop** if validity is maintained.

3. They **provide for guessing and elimination of responses.**

4. They **rely primarily upon recall and memory** and not problem solving and critical thinking.

## Short Answer and Recall Tests

The compromise between the multiple-choice test and the essay test is the short answer or the recall test. Short-answer questions can provide students with the opportunity to show their knowledge of a presentation, simulation, or analogy. They can be written to a specific item or point and thus do not require the time and effort involved in essay questions. They allow the student to use creativity and analysis that is not permissible with the multiple-choice test. The short answer and recall tests provide the instructor with the opportunity to pose simple questions or even completion questions. They provide the opportunity for expansion of creative ideas and expression of philosophies and opinions. They also provide the student with the opportunity to discuss unassigned material or materials they may have used on a research project or paper associated with the course. Short answer questions or recall questions may provide the student the opportunity to present the solution to problems or to develop hypothesis. Such questions may allow students to compare the differences between two statements, items or activities which is not possible in the use of many other tests.

### The Advantages of Recall Tests

The advantages of recall tests are:

1. They are **relatively simply to grade and construct**.

2. Recall questions **can address numerous areas and a broad field of content**.

3. They **require a specific recall** rather than a guess such as may occur in a true/false or multiple-choice.

### Disadvantages of Recall Tests

The disadvantages of recall tests include:

1. They may be **time consuming for the student** in terms of thinking and trying to recall something for which they have a mental block.

2. **Subjectivity may be introduced** due to similar responses.

3. It is **nearly impossible to measure analysis or synthesis** with these tests.

## True/False Tests

True/false questions are not commonly used at the college level any longer. Although they may have their place in a sampling of student responses or learning activity, they generally are not acceptable as being objective or valid. In the event there is opportunity for their use, the advantages, disadvantages and some suggestions are listed below.

### Advantages of True/False Questions

1. A large number of diverse questions may be asked on a specific topic.

2. They are good to stimulate students and give lower ability students a chance for success.

3. They are simple and time saving to develop.

4. They are valid as only two possible answers exist.

5. They are non-threatening and familiar to students.

6. They are easily scored.

### Disadvantages of True/False Questions

1. Even with the allowance for correction factors, true/false questions encourage guessing.

2. It is difficult to construct brief, complete true/false statements where the answer is not obvious.

3. Grading weight is equal for minor as well as significant items.

4. They are not appropriate for elaboration or discussion.

5. They tend to test the lower level of knowledge with no consideration for analysis and synthesis.

6. They are typically low in validity and reliability due to the guess factor.

### Constructing True/False Test Items

If you have elected to utilize true/false questions as part of your evaluation system, there are several factors to consider in the development of these questions. They are:

1. Avoid unclear statements with ambiguous words or "trick" questions.

2. Develop questions that require responses beyond the knowledge or rote memorization level.

3. Avoid patterning answers with a long string of trues or false or direct alteration.

4.  Avoid direct quotes as they will tip off responses.

5.  Avoid specific descriptors or adjectives that tip off responses.

## Grading

Grading is a major challenge for many new instructors and for more experienced ones too. Some instructors are harsh graders at the beginning to prove that they are not pushovers. Others are quite lenient. Grades reflect personal philosophy and human psychology as well as efforts to measure intellectual progress with standardized, objective criteria. Whatever our personal philosophy about grades, their importance to our students means that we must be fair and reasonable and maintain grading standards we can defend if challenged. Grades cause a lot of distress for undergraduates; this concern often seems to inhibit enthusiasm for learning for its own sake ("Do we have to know this for the exam?"), but grades are a fact of life. The good news is that they need not be counterproductive educationally if students know what to expect. Here are some general suggestions that can help to maintain fairness and consistency in our grading.

All of the elements of teaching (preparation, presentation and student activity) are reflected in the grading process. In addition, in an era of accountability, teachers are sometimes called upon to justify grades with documentation. Thus the establishment of firm criteria for grading is necessary. There are some general rules that are helpful in establishing the grading process. They are as follows:

1.  **Communicate criteria.** Faculty should communicate the grading criteria to be used the first or second session of class. A suggested chart for this activity is shown in figure 2 on page 155. Every effort should be made to allow students to respond to the grading format in the process, before the first evaluation is given.

2.  **Include criteria other than test scores.** Factors other than test scores should be included in the students' grades. This is especially true of social sciences courses where content criteria and problem solving is not easy

to assess. For example, if it is important for students to communicate or express ideas, then class participation *should* be a part of the grading criteria. If a paper or a project is part of the grade, students should be advised of the weight of the project applied to the grade. If laboratory demonstration is part of the course, the grade value should be made known.

3. **Avoid irrelevant factors.** Avoid introducing irrelevant factors to the grading process. Including attendance and tardiness in the grading criteria is unwise. Many experienced teachers feel that if students possess knowledge and show that they have reached the objectives of the course, they should be evaluated on that criteria only. The insistence that students should sit in the room for a certain number of minutes to hear things they already know may be unrealistic. This is especially true when teaching adults who may have significant career and business experience but have not received the official credit or coursework. Introducing attendance in class as part of the grading criteria simply breeds animosity with students and is very difficult for the instructor to justify.

4. **Weigh grading criteria carefully.** Be careful not to weight certain segments of the grading criteria inappropriately. For example, if you are to develop a grading plan such as shown in the diagram in figure 2, and then allow 90% of the grade to count as the final examination, you have probably defeated the purpose of comprehensive grading. Equally important is the weighing of extra credit for extra work. If such a technique is used it should not penalize students who do not feel it necessary to do extra work.

5. **Grade students on their achievement, not on other students.** Grading should be based upon the criteria of the course objectives and not upon other students' scores. Many years ago, teachers used the technique of "grad-

ing on the curve." This technique essentially distributed
all students and all classes on a normal bell curve and
determined the percentage of A's, B's, C's, and D's. This
placed students in competition with each other rather
than cooperating in the learning experience. The practice
has been abandoned in the modern classroom. In recent
years, criterion-based grading has found favor. Criterion-
based grading evaluates students independent of other
students based upon the criteria of the course. The criteria of the course are the objectives written for the course.
Thus, quite simply the student should be graded upon the
degree upon which they have completed the objectives
of the course and not how other students achieve. Thus,
if all students reach all objectives they all should receive
passing grades.

## Evaluation Plan

In order to clearly delineate criteria for assignment of grades, it is
helpful if you first develop an evaluation plan. An evaluation plan is
a very simple device used to develop a short worksheet form. The
plan contains all of the factors that apply to the evaluation of the
students. Across from these factors is listed a percentage of weight
that will be assigned to various factors. A third column indicates the
points received for each factor. A sample plan is shown in figure 2.

*Evaluation Chart*

| Grade Factors | Percentage of Final Grade | Possible Points | Points Received |
|---|---|---|---|
| Tests | 60 | 90 | |
| Paper | 20 | 30 | |
| Project | 10 | 15 | |
| Class Participation | 10 | 15 | |
| | | | |
| TOTALS | 100 | 150 | |

*Figure 2—Evaluation Chart Sample*

Please note that any number of factors can be included in the first
column. For example, a technical course might include laboratory
work, laboratory demonstrations or completion of projects. An

evaluation worksheet allows you to weight factors that apply to a specific class with the flexibility of changing them when necessary. Obviously when developing the chart, it is necessary that the weight total 100% for the course. In order to complete the evaluation worksheet, you must simply assign the number of points possible to each of the categories. Keep in mind that the total number of points may not equal 100, depending upon the application involved. (Example shows 150.) It remains then to simply add a fourth column titled "points received". Points received, obviously, are the number of points earned by the student in each category.

This system allows you the flexibility of established documented criteria for the assignment of grades. You may, for example, arbitrarily put the total number of points desired to equal 100%. This then can be converted to the number of points necessary to be earned through each of the factors by multiplying by the percentage. An additional step is to simply take that number of points divided by the number of activities in each of the factors to determine the value for each activity, even to the level of determining the value of each test question. This documentation clearly indicates to the students the process by which evaluation is conducted in a business-like and professional manner.

**Dr. Don Greive** *is an author/editor and consultant for adjunct faculty professional development programs.*

*In Their Own Words*

"In Their Own Words" essays are written by administrators, tenured and non-tenured faculty members who work at a variety of two- and four-year colleges and universities. We are grateful to these educators for sharing their insights and their expertise.

## Halving the Paperwork and Doubling the Fun

A concern of teaching faculty is how to make class interesting, exciting and meaningful while keeping instructor workload to a reasonable level. If you are too tired to correct mounds of papers at night, try this three-step approach. It will keep you and your students stimulated and save you time. It will enable you to reach, and therefore teach, all the students in your course.

As an instructor of educational psychology, I tell my students that in this course they will learn self-direction, a skill that they can carry with them their entire lives. This process minimizes the amount of time it takes to prepare (and later revise) my syllabus while empowering the students and encouraging critical thinking and problem-solving skills. I use the following three-step model which I hope will help you.

First, rather than requiring a standard research report—which takes hours of your time to correct—allow students to produce a project in the form of art, music, poetry, a play, or the more traditional presentation mode of the paper.

For you, this takes away from feeling overwhelmed when a big stack of papers is before you, awaiting correction. It lets you evaluate in a more relaxed mode—on your couch with your feet propped up, watching student-produced videos. You save time by listening to student-produced audio tapes while driving in the car, just be sure to keep a tape recorder in your car to record your comments on each audio presentations.

For the students, their different styles are acknowledged, and they are allowed to express themselves in whatever mode works best for them. They are allowed to showcase their talents. In addition, students like this approach because they are given a choice, and therefore some control, in the class.

Second, have the whole class develop rubrics to be used for evaluation. Encourage them to make the rubrics as specific as possible. Be sure that this evaluation tool can be used for products that are not standard papers. For example, will the rubric work for a piece of art the student has done as well as it will for a standard paper?

Examples of guidelines include:

1.  Is there evidence that the material was read/viewed/listened to and understood?

2.  Did the student explain why the material is important to know?

3.  Did the student connect the material to previous classroom and outside learning?

4.  Does it show good organization and reflective thinking?

For you, this saves time. The process takes one to two hours. These are hours for which you do not have to prepare. Also, because they have developed the rubric, your students are less likely to complain about any possible unfairness in your grading.

For students, this process encourages critical thinking and problem solving, giving them important life skills. They will perform better on their assignments because they really know what is expected of them. After all, they developed the expectations.

Third, use a three-part assessment for the assignment: self-evaluation, peer evaluation, and instructor evaluation. Have students evaluate their own work according to the rubric the class developed.

The student only puts the numeral you have assigned to them (rather than their name) on their product to assure anonymity and objectivity for the next part, review by the peer evaluators. Randomly distribute the products to pairs of students who work together to evaluate two products according to the rubric. Ask the students to make comments, to give as much feedback as possible. The original author now has the option of redoing the product based on the feedback he or she received from their peer evaluators.

Finally, one week later, collect the finished products for your evaluation. If a student does not wish to redo his or her product, that is her/his choice. I find, however, that most students welcome the chance to improve their work before a grade is given, especially when the improvements are easy to fix, such as correcting spelling errors.

For you, correcting students' work becomes easier since you are correcting polished products rather than work which, in the past, became tedious to correct because of myriad mechanical errors (spelling, punctuation, etc.). The peer evaluation process takes approximately one hour—another hour for which you do not have to prepare.

For the students, this process helps them develop better written language skills. They like it because it gives them a "second chance."

The resulting empowerment generated by this student-centered curriculum, instruction, and evaluation model demonstrates the importance of student-centered learning. It allows you, as an adjunct instructor, to adapt various learning styles, to reach—and therefore teach—every student in your course. And it makes your job easier and more enjoyable.

*Contributed by:* **Rea H. Kirk** *of University of Wisconsin-Platteville, Platteville, WI.*

# References

Abington-Cooper, M., & Holmes, G. (2000). "Pedagogy vs. Andragogy: A False Dichotomy?" *The Journal of Technology Studies*, Summer/Fall, Volume 26.

Angelo, T. A. & Cross, K. P. (1993*). Classroom assessment techniques a handbook for college teachers.* San Francisco, CA: Jossey-Bass Publishers.

Astin, A. and Oseguera, L. "The Declining 'Equity' of American Education." *The Review of higher Education*, Vol. 27 No. 3, pages 321-341, Spring 2004.

Bastedo, Michael N. and Patricia J. Gumport. (2003). "Access to What?: Mission Differentiation and Academic Stratification in U. S. Public Higher Education." *Higher Education: The International Journal of Higher Education and Educational Planning* 46: 341-359.

Beardsley, M. (1975). *Thinking straight*. Englewood Cliffs, NJ: Prentice-Hall.

Beck, E. (2011) *Going the Distance: A Handbook for Part-Time & Adjunct Faculty Who Teach Online*. Ann Arbor, MI: Part-Time Press.

Bligh, D. (2000*). What's the Use of Lectures?* San Francisco, CA: Jossey-Bass Publishers.

Boettcher, J. V. (1999). Copyright and intellectual property. *Syllabus,* 34-36.

Brookfield, S. (2011). *Teaching for Critical Thinking*. San Francisco, CA: Jossey-Bass Publishers.

Browne M. & Keeley, S. (2014). *Asking the right questions: A guide to critical thinking*. Englewood Cliffs NJ: Prentice-Hall.

Burgess, Larry A., Samuels, Carl. (1999). "Impact of Full-Time Versus Part-Time Instructor Status on College Student Retention and Academic Performance." *Community College Journal of Research and Practice*, 23:5, 487-498.

Burgstahler, S., & Cory, R. (2008). *Universal design in higher education: From principles to practice*. Cambridge, Mass: Harvard Education Press.

Chaffee, J. (2014). *Thinking critically.* New York, NY: Cengage Learning

Community College Survey of Student Engagement (2012*).* Center for Community College Student Engagement, University of Texas-Austin.

Collins, M. (2011). *Teaching in the Sciences: A Handbook for Part-Time & Adjunct Faculty.* Ann Arbor, MI: The Part-Time Press.

Cooper, J., Robinson P. (2014). "Implementing Small-Group Instruction: Insights from Successful Practitioners." *New Directions for Teaching and Learning,* Volume 2000, Issue 81, pages 63–76, Spring 2000.

Cooper, J., Robinson, P. (1998). "Small group instruction: An annotated bibliography of science, mathematics, engineering, and technology resources in higher education (Occasional Paper No. 6)." Madison: University of Wisconsin-Madison, National Institute for Science Education.

Cross, K. P. (1981). *Adults as learners.* San Francisco, CA: Jossey-Bass.

*Creating a positive learning environment.* (1998) Toronto: Humber College of Applied Arts and Technology.

Cyrs, T. E. (1997). "Competence in teaching at a distance." *Teaching and learning at a distance: What it takes to effectively to design, deliver and evaluate programs.* San Francisco: Jossey-Bass.

deFrondville, Tristan. (2009). "Ten Steps to Better Student Engagement." EPIC. http://www.epiconline.org/download/38101/

Davenport, J., & Davenport, J. A. (1985). "A chronology and analysis of the andragogy debate." *Adult Educational Quarterly*, 35 (3), 152159.

Davis, B. G. (2009). *Tools for teaching.* San Francisco, CA: Jossey-Bass Publishers.

Dworetzky, J. & Davis, N. (1995). *Human development: A lifespan approach, 2nd ed.* New York, NY: West Publishing Co.

Elias, J. M. (1979). "Andragogy Revisited." *Adult Education Quarterly*, June vol. 29 no. 4, 252-256.

Ertmer, P. and Gopalakrishnan, S. and Ross, E. (2001). "Comparing Perceptions of Exemplary Technology Use to Best Practice." *Journal of Research on Computing in Education*, 33-5.

Fletcher, A. (2009) "Meaningful student involvement: Guide to students as partners in school change." Olympia, WA: *CommonAction*. p. 4.

Freeman, J. (1993). *Thinking logically.* Englewood Cliffs, NJ: Prentice-Hall.

Govier, T. (1988). *Selected issues in logic and communication.* Belmont, CA: Wadsworth.

Gross Davis, Barbara. (2009). "Diversity and Complexity in the Classroom: Considerations of Race, Ethnicity and Gende." *Tools for Teaching, 2nd Ed.* San Francisco: Jossey-Bass.

Hartman, J. L. & Truman B. E. (1997). "Going virtual: Lessons learned." Paper presented at the CAUSE '97 Conference, Orlando, FL.

Hartree, A. (1984). "Malcolm Knowles' theory of andragogy: A critique." *International Journal of Lifelong Education*, 3, 203-210.

Hew, K. F and Brush, T. (2007). "Integrating technology into K-12 teaching and learning: current knowledge gaps and recommendations for future research." *Educational Technology Research and Development*, 55-3, 223-252.

Inside Iowa State, *Iowa State University, Ames IA.*

Jacoby, Daniel (2006). "Effects of Part-Time Faculty Employment on Community College Graduate Rates." *The Journal of Higher Education,* 77(6):1081-1103.

Jones, Richard D. (2008) "Strengthening Student Engagement." International Center for Leadership in Education. Retrieved 6/10/16 from http://www.cesdp.nmhu.edu/

Kahane, H. (2013). *Logic and contemporary rhetoric.* New York, NY: Cengage Learning.

Knowles, M. (1990). *The adult learner-A neglected species.* Houston, TX: Gulf Publishing Co.

Knowles, M. (1980). *The Modern Practice of Adult Education: From Pedagogy and Andragogy.* New York, NY: Cambridge.

Kruse, K. (2009). "Gagne's nine events of instruction: An introduction." Retrieved on September 28, 2015 from: http://citt.ufl.edu/tools/gagnes-9-events-of-instruction/

Lawless, K. A., and Pellegrino, J. W. (2007). "Professional Development in Integrating Technology Into Teaching and Learning: Knowns, Unknowns, and Ways to Pursue Better Questions and Answers." *Review of Educational Research*, 77-4, 575.

Lindbeck, R. and Fodrey, B. (2012). "Integrating Technology into the College Classroom: Current Practices and Future Opportunities." *National Social Science Technology Journal*, Volume 1-1.

London, J. (1973). "Adult education for the 1970's: Promise or illusion?" *Adult Education*, 24 (1), 60-70.

MacGregor, J. (1990). "Collaborative learning: Shared inquiry as a process of reform" In Svinicki, M. D. (Ed.), The changing face of college teaching, *New Directions for Teaching and Learning* No. 42.

McKeachie, W. J. et. al. (2010). *Teaching tips strategies, research, and theory for college and university teachers*. Boston, MA: Wadsworth Publishing.

McKenzie, L. (1979). "A response to Elias." *Adult Education*, 29 (4), 256-260.

Mishra, P., and Koehler, M. J. (2006). "Technological Pedagogical Content Knowledge: A Framework for Teacher Knowledge." Teachers *College Record*, 108-6, 1017-1054.

Missimer, C. (1990). *Good arguments: An introduction to critical thinking*. Englewood Cliffs, NJ: Prentice-Hall.

Mohring, P. M. (1989). "Andragogy and pedagogy: A comment on their erroneous usage" (Training and Development Research Center Project No. 21). St. Paul, MN: Department of Vocational and Technical Education, Minnesota University.

National Center for Education Statistics (NCES), 2011. "Students with Disabilities at Degree-Granting Postsecondary Institutions." U.S. Department of Education. Washington, DC: U.S. Government Printing Office. Retrieved from: http://nces.ed.gov/pubs2011/2011018.pdf.

National Center for Education Statistics (NCES), 2006. "The Condition of Education, 2006." U.S. Department of Education. Washington, DC: U.S. Government Printing Office. Retrieved from: http://nces.ed.gov/programs/coe/index.asp.

New England Literacy Resource Center (2010). "Drivers of Persistence." Retrieved July 7, 2016, from http://www.nelrc.org/persist/drivers.html.

Palmer, P. J. (2007). *The courage to teach exploring the inner landscape of a teacher's life.* San Francisco, CA: Jossey-Bass Publishers.

President and Fellows of Harvard College (2010). Derek Bok Center for Teaching and Learning, Harvard University. http://isites.harvard.edu/fs/html/icb.topic58474/TFTlectures.html.

Pope, Justin (2014). "What Are MOOCs Good For?" *MIT Technology Review*, Dec. 15, 2014.

Pryor, J.H., Hurtado, S., DeAngelo, L., Palucki Blake, L., & Tran, S., (2014). "The American freshman: National norms Fall 2014." Los Angeles: Higher Education Research Institute, UCLA. http://www.heri.ucla.edu/monographs/theamericanfreshman2014.pdf

Pryor, J.H., Hurtado, S., DeAngelo, L., Palucki Blake, L., & Tran, S., (2010). "The American freshman: National norms Fall 2010." Los Angeles: Higher Education Research Institute, UCLA. http://www.heri.ucla.edu/PDFs/pubs/briefs/HERI_ResearchBrief_Norms2010.pdf

Pryor, J.H., Hurtado, S., (2009). "The American Freshman: Forty Year Trends." Los Angeles: Higher Education Research Institute, UCLA. http://heri.ucla.edu/40yrtrends.php

Pryor, J.H., Hurtado, S., (2008). "The American Freshman: Forty Year Trends." Los Angeles: Higher Education Research Institute, UCLA. http://heri.ucla.edu/40yrtrends.php

Rachal, J. R. (1994). "Andragogical and pedagogical methods compared: A review of the experimental literature (Report)." Hattisburg: University of Southern Mississippi. (ERIC Document Reproduction Service No. ED 380 566)

Raines, C. (2003). "Managing Millennials." In Connecting generations : the sourcebook for a new workplace. Menlo Park, Ca. Crisp Publications.

Riegel, K. (1973). "Dialectical operations: The final period of cognitive development." *Human Development, (16),* 346-370.

Rockwood, H. S. III (1995a). "Cooperative and collaborative learning" The national teaching & learning forum, 4 (6), 8-9.

Rockwood, H. S. III (1995b). "Cooperative and collaborative learning" The national teaching & learning forum, 5 (1), 8-10.

Seech, Z. (2004) *Open minds and everyday reasoning.* Belmont, CA: Wadsworth.

Sego, A. (1996). *Cooperative learning-A classroom guide.* Elyria, OH: Info-Tec.

Selwyn, N. (2007). "The use of computer technology in university teaching and learning: a critical perspective." *Journal of Computer Assisted Learning,* 23, 83-94.

Seymour, D. & Beardslee, E. (1990). *Critical thinking activities.* Palo Alto, CA: Seymour Publications.

Shulman, L. (1986). "Those Who Understand: Knowledge Growth in Teaching.*" Educational Researcher,* Vol. 15, No. 2, pp. 4-14.

Singh, R., & Means, B. (2000). "Effects of Technology on Classrooms and Students. U.S. Department of Education Office of Educational Research & Improvement." Retrieved November 28, 2015, from http://www2.ed.gov/pubs/EdReformStudies/EdTech/effectsstudents.html

Smaldino, S. & Simonson, M.. (2014). *Teaching and Learning at a Distance: Foundations of Distance Education, 6th Edition.* San Francisco, CA:  Information Age Publishing.

Smith, B. L., & MacGregor, J. T. (1992). "What is collaborative learning?" In Goodsell, A. S., Maher, M. R., Smith, B. L., & MacGregor, J. (Eds), *Collaborative Learning: A Sourcebook for Higher Education.*

Soluski, K. & Vai M. (2015 ).*Essentials of Online Course Design: A Standards-Based Guide (Essentials of Online Learning) 2nd Edition*. New York, NY: Routledge.

Strauss, W. and Howe, N. (2007). *Millennials go to college, 2nd Ed.* Great Falls, VA: Life Course Associates.

Surry, D. and Land, S. (2000). "Strategies for Motivating Higher Education Faculty to Use Technology." *Innovations in Education and Training International*, 37-2, 145-153.

Tucker, R. (1997). "Less than critical thinking, Part I." *Adult Assessment Forum VI* (3), 3-6.

Umbach, Paul. D. (2008). "The effects of part-time faculty appointments on instructional techniques and commitment to teaching." Paper Presented at the 33rd Annual Conference of the Association for the Study of Higher Education.

University of Maryland Center for Teaching Excellence. (2013). "Large Classes: A Teaching Guide." http://www.cte.umd.edu/library/teachingLargeClass/guide/index.html

Vella, J. (2007). "Interactivity: From agents to outcomes." *On Teaching and Learning: Putting the Principles and Practices of Dialogue Education into Action*. San Francisco, CA: Jossey-Bass Publishers.

Wagner, E.D. (1997). "Interactivity: From agents to outcomes." In T. E. Cyres (Ed.), Teaching and learning at a distance: What it takes to effectively design, deliver and evaluate programs: *New directions for teaching and learning* (pp. 19-26) San Francisco: Jossey-Bass.

Westerman, J. (1995-1996). "Teaching Excellence: TOWARD THE BEST IN THE ACADEMY," Vol. 7, No.8, 1995-1996.

Wulff D. H., Nyquist J. D., Abbott R. D. (1987). "Students' perceptions of large classes." In: Weimer M.G., editor. *Teaching Large Classes Well. New Directions for Teaching and Learning*. San Francisco, CA: Jossey-Bass Publishers.

# Index

## Symbols

## A

## B

## Q

## R

## W

## X

## Y